RICHARD II

RICHARD II

William Shakespeare

Edited by
CEDRIC WATTS

WORDSWORTH CLASSICS

For my husband
ANTHONY JOHN RANSON
with love from your wife, the publisher.
Eternally grateful for your unconditional love.

Readers who are interested in other titles from
Wordsworth Editions are invited to visit our website at
www.wordsworth-editions.com

This edition first published in 2012 by
Wordsworth Editions Limited
8B East Street, Ware, Hertfordshire SG12 9HJ

ISBN   978 1 84022 720 8

Wordsworth Editions
is the company founded in 1987 by
MICHAEL TRAYLER

Typeset in Great Britain by Antony Gray
Printed and bound by Clays Ltd, St Ives plc

CONTENTS

GENERAL INTRODUCTION

In the Wordsworth Classics' Shakespeare Series, the inaugural volumes, *Romeo and Juliet*, *The Merchant of Venice* and *Henry V*, have been followed by *The Taming of the Shrew*, *Richard II*, *A Midsummer Night's Dream*, *Much Ado about Nothing*, *Julius Cæsar*, *Hamlet*, *Twelfth Night*, *Measure for Measure*, *Othello*, *Macbeth*, *King Lear*, *Antony and Cleopatra*, *The Winter's Tale* and *The Tempest*. Each play in this Shakespeare Series is accompanied by a standard apparatus, including an introduction, explanatory notes and a glossary. The textual editing takes account of recent scholarship, while giving the material a careful reappraisal. The apparatus is, however, concise rather than elaborate. We hope that the resultant volumes prove to be handy, reliable and helpful. Above all, we hope that, from Shakespeare's works, readers will derive pleasure, wisdom, provocations, challenges, and insights: insights into his culture and ours, and into the era of civilisation to which his writings have made (and continue to make) such potently influential contributions. Shakespeare's eloquence will, undoubtedly, re-echo 'in states unborn and accents yet unknown'.

CEDRIC WATTS
Series Editor

INTRODUCTION

'Must! It is somewhat hard when kings must go.'[1]

I

Richard II is one of Shakespeare's finest works: lucid, eloquent, and intelligently structured. To a large extent, it shifts and changes according to the observer's viewpoint and the context in which it is observed. The work can be regarded as a tragedy, or a history play, or a political drama, or as one part of a vast dramatic cycle which helped to generate England's national identity. Today, to some of us, *Richard II* may appear conservative, but in 1601, to powerful people, it seemed subversive.

Although it is usually termed one of Shakespeare's Histories, *Richard II* was originally registered, in 1597, as *The Tragedie of Richard the Second*; and the First Quarto, issued in the same year, was entitled *The Tragedie of King Richard the second*.[2] Just as an individual can be related to two and more families, so can a literary work. If you think of *Richard II* as a history play, questions of factual accuracy and political distortion then come to mind. Think of it as a tragedy, and it will invite comparison with such classical works as *Agamemnon*, *King Œdipus* and *The Bacchae*. In *Richard II*, as in all three of these ancient plays, we see a ruler who is tainted by arrogance and fecklessly ignores good advice, but, in his downfall, becomes a sympathetic object of concern. The main plot thus displays a familiar pattern of tragic irony.

Among *genres* of literature, a tragedy is a literary work which dramatises admirably a sequence of events which focuses moral attention on human suffering. (The term 'a tragedy' often has an honorific implication; as, if the work did not 'dramatise admirably' such a sequence, a term lacking prestige could be used: 'a melodrama' or 'Grand Guignol', perhaps.) For Chaucer's Monk, in The Canterbury Tales, a tragedy told a simple exemplary story: that of a person who stands in an eminent position and enjoys prosperity but falls into misery and ends wretchedly. The moral: put your trust not in this unreliable world but in the prospect of heaven for the virtuous. In 1904, however, A. C. Bradley, writing in Shakespearean Tragedy, declared that 'tragedy would not be tragedy if it were not a painful mystery'.[3] There, modern agnosticism seems to have influenced the concept: instead of being morally and theologically specific, tragedy hints at profound mysteries but eschews the didactic. In the Elizabethan Age, dramatists depicting a tragic protagonist were pulled between a traditional sense of the exemplary case and a more modern sense of the value of complexity and ambiguity. In Richard II, our view of Richard probably shifts from one of disgust, when he cynically welcomes Gaunt's death, to one of pity or sympathy as he is encompassed by enemies and becomes the introspective victim. Meanwhile, numerous speeches offer us moral and theological interpretations of the events.

If you know Christopher Marlowe's play Edward II, you may gain a particularly strong déjà-vu feeling: in character, Richard seems more like Edward's twin brother than his great-grandson. Richard II was probably written in 1595, and Marlowe had been killed in 1593; so, where there are similarities implying debts, any debts are of Shakespeare to Marlowe. And debts do seem to be conspicuous. Geoffrey Bullough summarises some of the evidence when comparing the two works:

> Both are plays about the same dynasty, and the reign of Richard II repeats themes apparent in the earlier one. Edward II was the unworthy successor of the conquering Edward I. So Richard II was the unworthy successor of his grandfather Edward III (Edward II's son). Edward II failed to conquer Scotland as Richard failed in Ireland. In the plays about them both appear as weak rulers, capricious and arbitrary, who alienate their wiser counsellors and listen to favourites. In each play the favourites number three (Gaveston, Spencer and Baldock in Edward II). In each play a Duke of Lancaster warns the king (in vain) . . . Act I in each piece shows the king at odds with many of his nobles about a banishment . . . In both plays the king is deposed, ill-

treated, and then murdered in an interesting manner, leaving the kingdom in the hands of a better ruler. In each the King becomes more likeable in defeat than he was in power, and the play becomes an experiment in counterpointing the tragedy of a weak and erring central figure against the conflict of opposing groups . . . [4]

We could add that each king marries a French princess called Isabella (or Isabelle); but Richard's male favourites are accused of leading him astray sexually:

> You have, in manner, with your sinful hours,
> Made a divorce betwixt his Queen and him,
> Broke the possession of a royal bed[;].

and, in Marlowe's play, Edward certainly has a stronger sexual and emotional relationship with his male favourite, Gaveston, than with his queen. The courts of both kings are tainted by decadence and susceptible to foreign (particularly Italian) fashions. 'Englishness', in contrast, is associated with patriotism, plain clothing, courage and manliness.

As Marlowe's Edward II loses power, he becomes a self-pitying, self-dramatising and introspective figure. So, too, does Richard II. Indeed, there are times when their personalities seem interchangeable. When Edward is obliged to hand over the crown, he is variously suppliant, defiant, arrogant and pitiable:

> Here, take my crown; the life of Edward too:
> *Taking off the crown.*
> Two kings in England cannot reign at once.
> But stay a while. Let me be king till night,
> That I may gaze upon this glittering crown;
> So shall my eyes receive their last content,
> My head, the latest honour due to it,
> And jointly both yield up their wishèd right.
> Continue ever, thou celestial sun;
> Let never silent night possess this clime;
> Stand still, you watches of the element;
> All times and seasons, rest you at a stay,

That Edward may be still fair England's king!
But day's bright beams doth vanish fast away,
And needs I must resign my wishèd crown.
Inhuman creatures, nurs'd with tiger's milk,
Why gape you for your sovereign's overthrow?
My diadem, I mean, and guiltless life.
See, monsters, see! I'll wear my crown again.
> *Putting on the crown.*
What, fear you not the fury of your king?
But, hapless Edward, thou art fondly led;
They pass not for thy frowns as late they did.[5]

The combination of poetic eloquence with fluctuations in mood
and tone shows that Marlowe was at the forefront of literary
experimentation, bringing new complexity to characterisation.
And experiments like this were closely observed by Shakespeare.
Thus his Richard, also forced to recognise the waning of his
power and to hand over the crown, responds with similar
emotional volatility, and consults a mirror, an action symbolising
both truth-seeking and vanity.

O, that I were a mockery-king of snow,
Standing before the sun of Bullingbrooke,
To melt myself away in water-drops.
Good King, great King, and yet not greatly good;
And if my word be sterling yet in England,
Let it command a mirror hither straight,
That it may show me what a face I have,
Since it is bankrupt of his majesty . . .
Give me that glass, and therein will I read.
> [*He studies his reflection.*
No deeper wrinkles yet? Hath sorrow struck
So many blows upon this face of mine,
And made no deeper wounds? O flatt'ring glass,
Like to my followers in prosperity,
Thou dost beguile me. Was this face the face
That every day, under his household roof,
Did keep ten thousand men? Was this the face
That like the sun did make beholders wink?

Was this the face that faced so many follies,
And was at last out-faced by Bullingbrooke?
A brittle glory shineth in this face;
As brittle as the glory is the face —
[*He hurls the mirror down, smashing it.*

Again, there are fluctuations in mood and tone (now complicated by the ebullient word-play). As if to underline the Marlovian heritage, here part of Richard's rhetoric clearly echoes two of the most famous lines in Marlowe's *Doctor Faustus*, in Faustus's address to the imagined Helen of Troy:

Was this the face that launched a thousand ships,
And burned the topless towers of Ilium? [6]

What both those long speeches epitomise is the central paradox which is exploited in the tradition of 'regal tragedy'. A king may be semi-divine, God's deputy on earth, judgeable by the Lord alone; but a king is, inevitably, fallible, vulnerable, subject to envy and rebellion, and ultimately mortal. Of course, one could write a tragedy about a bored housewife or a travelling salesman: Ibsen's *Hedda Gabler* and Arthur Miller's *Death of a Salesman* proved that point. In regal tragedy, however, the exalted status of the vulnerable monarch serves to magnify the social consequences of a familiar disparity which probably lurks within most of us. This is a disparity between the greater self we can imagine and the humdrum self that we usually inhabit. In a perishable carcase, a mediocre person may harbour exalted and perhaps immortal longings. When King Richard falls, however, others fall with him, some of them to their deaths. Sometimes, for Richard, the sense that he is a mere mortal is dominant:

[T]hrow away respect,
Tradition, form, and ceremonious duty;
For you have but mistook me all this while:
I live with bread like you, feel want,
Taste grief, need friends: subjected thus,
How can you say to me, I am a king?

At other times, his sense of semi-divinity prevails:

> Not all the water in the rough rude sea
> Can wash the balm from an anointed king.
> The breath of worldly men cannot dispose
> The deputy elected by the Lord.
> For every man that Bullingbrooke hath pressed
> To lift shrewd steel against our golden crown,
> God for his Richard hath in heavenly pay
> A glorious angel; then, if angels fight,
> Weak men must fall, for heaven still guards the right.

'Yet looks he like a king', remarks York, when Richard stands at bay; and Richard, even as he dies, asserts (in ritualising couplets) his royalty and his heavenly destiny:

> Exton, thy fierce hand
> Hath with the King's blood stained the King's own land.
> – Mount, mount, my soul; thy seat is up on high,
> Whilst my gross flesh sinks downward, here to die.

If, in the early part of the play, Richard seems callous, feckless and cynical, it is in his downfall that his consciousness of his rôle as God's deputy gathers force. The contrast with Marlowe's treatment of history here becomes obvious. The similarities between *Richard II* and *Edward II* naturally give prominence to the differences. Shakespeare's play has a sustained eloquence and a lyrical richness lacking from Marlowe's. In *Richard II* (providing evidence that this work is contemporaneous with *Romeo and Juliet* and *Love's Labour's Lost*), linguistic wit flourishes: punning, simile-seeking and ambiguity-teasing abound; so that even the Queen's grief generates paradoxes involving a 'heavy nothing' which yet begets something (2.2.28–40). Such paronomasia is relatively sparse in *Edward II*. Another difference is that Shakespeare's play offers a wider range of individuated characters than does Marlowe's. An important theme lacking from *Edward II* is that of England as 'demi-Eden': a potentially paradisal realm. The religious dimension of patriotic politics engages Shakespeare's magination but seems alien to Marlowe's more sceptical temperament. If the England of

Richard II is termed by Gaunt a demi-Eden, Richard's downfall is 'a second Fall of cursèd man', and the monarch even compares himself to the betrayed Christ – though Jesus was betrayed by only one Judas. After Richard's death, his sacred dimension gains increasing warranty. Bullingbrooke curses the killer, Exton: 'With Cain go wander through the shades of night'; and then promises to undertake a pilgrimage to purge his own guilt:

> I'll make a voyage to the Holy Land,
> To wash this blood off from my guilty hand.

It is a voyage which he never has the leisure to make, and this is partly because he is beset by political and familial worries. God, it may seem, is avenging the betrayed and murdered Richard. As in the ancient tragedies of Aeschylus, Sophocles and Euripides, the fate of the tragic protagonist evokes the problem of theodicy: the theological problem of reconciling the fact of human suffering with the notion that the world is governed by a just God or by just gods. Historically, complex tragedy emerges when traditional religious beliefs are challenged by new scepticism. Tragedy then aspires to resolve as paradox the conflict between human hope and humiliating fact.

2

Though *Richard II* can be appraised as a tragedy, in 1623 it was classified as a History Play. The classification was made by two of Shakespeare's colleagues when, seven years after his death, they produced the First Folio, the first 'collected edition' of Shakespeare's works. That generic categorisation was entirely reasonable, for Shakespeare had based the play on various chronicles which, with varying degrees of historical accuracy, told the story of Richard's reign. An important source was the second edition (1587) of a work by Raphael Holinshed and others, *Chronicles of England, Scotland and Ireland*. From this work Shakespeare selected a great deal of material, ranging from the large (main events in the last two years of Richard's life) to the small (strange and vivid details). He noted the ironies of familial division: the sons of King Edward III included John of Gaunt, Edmund (Duke of York) and Thomas Woodstock (Duke of

Gloucester). Edward's grandson, Richard II (son of the Black
Prince), would lethally oppose Woodstock while alienating two
other uncles, Edmund and John of Gaunt.

As usual, however, Shakespeare took considerable liberties with
the historical accounts. For instance, in the play a poignant
character is Richard's queen, Isabella. She appears in several scenes,
a worried, devoted, loving and spirited wife. In Act 5, scene 1, her
parting from Richard is movingly protracted, modulating from the
relatively realistic, as she urges him to show more courage and
defiance, to the lyrically stylised, as their last loving farewell
becomes a duet in rhyming couplets. The real queen, however,
was no woman but a child. She was born on 9 November 1389, he
on 6 January 1367. Therefore, at the time of their marriage by
proxy on 12 March 1396, Richard was twenty-nine and Isabella
was six; and, at his death, he was thirty-three and she ten.[7] This
gross disparity in ages was subordinated to diplomatic and dynastic
expedience. In the interests of dramatic poignancy and political
prudence, Shakespeare chooses to conceal the truth.

Here is another instance. In Act 5, scene 2, the Duchess of York
vividly expresses her anxieties as mother of her imperilled son,
Aumerle. She laments that if he were to be executed for treason,
she is too old to bear her husband another heir. This contributes to
a fine scene of familial conflict, and thus forms part of the theme
of 'divided families' which will extend far into this tetralogy.
Historically, however, the mother of Aumerle was not this Duchess
of York at all but her predecessor, the Duke's first wife; and
Aumerle was not the sole son, for he had both a sister and a brother.

Shakespeare's John of Gaunt is famously a romantic patriot,
extolling the splendour of England and denouncing the misrule by
Richard. You wouldn't guess from the play that the historic John of
Gaunt had been a highly unpopular magnate. When Gaunt had
gained domination of Edward III's parliament in 1376–7, for
example, he had headed a coalition containing corrupt household
servants, courtiers and officials which undid much of the previous
administration's good work against corruption, and the courageous
Speaker of the House of Commons was imprisoned. Gaunt was
then 'the best hated man in England'. During the Peasants' Revolt
(1381), the rebels destroyed his palace, the Savoy, in London.[8]
Shakespeare chooses to idealise his Gaunt, giving him a powerfully

choric function. Later, the 'garden' imagery of Gaunt's 'sceptred isle' speech ('This earth of majesty . . . This blessèd plot') will resonate in Act 3, scene 4, in the speech by the remarkably knowledgeable and homiletic gardener: an invented character who, again, serves as a choric commentator. Overshadowing the play's intrigues is the late Duke of Gloucester, Woodstock, the 'plain well-meaning soul' whose death (instigated by Richard) is repeatedly the occasion of angry disputes. Shakespeare gives no hint that in 1387 the real Duke of Gloucester had led the Lords Appellant, a rebellious band of powerful noblemen who had, for a while, seized power from Richard and executed his main supporters.[9] Gradually, Richard reasserted himself; but in 1399 came his downfall.

Shakespeare's play follows Lancastrian chroniclers in showing a Richard who submits to Bullingbrooke and agrees to abdicate. The historical facts appear to be that Richard, deceived by Bullingbrooke (who had sworn that he had no designs on the throne), was treacherously ambushed and captured by forces loyal to the usurper, and thereafter kept prisoner until his death.[10] Richard did not abdicate in person before a full audience in the Palace of Westminster. He remained imprisoned, while the assembly heard the reading of a document of abdication which Richard was said to have signed. In the play, Richard finally goes down fighting: he valiantly kills two of his numerous assailants before being slain himself. Certainly, one of the early chroniclers stated that Richard was hacked to death, on Bullingbrooke's orders, by a gang of eight led by Exton. Centuries later, however, when Richard's skeleton was exhumed, it bore no marks of violence. Modern historians therefore give more credence to the versions offered by other chroniclers, which are that Richard either starved himself to death or was deliberately starved by his captors (the latter option being far more plausible).[11] Clearly, Shakespeare's choice gives the play a more dramatic climax and, again, helps to win sympathy for Richard by showing that though, when formerly in adversity, he was inclined to reflect rather than act, in this final desperate emergency he can act with courage and pride.

Ernest Schanzer once wrote a book on three 'problem plays' by Shakespeare: *Julius Cæsar*, *Measure for Measure* and *Antony and Cleopatra*. He said that a problem play has a central moral problem which is presented in such a way that we are uncertain of our moral bearings, 'so that uncertain and divided responses to it in the minds of the audience are possible or even probable'. In such works, the dramatist may employ 'dramatic coquetry', 'manipulating our response to the principal characters, playing fast and loose with our affections for them, engaging and alienating them in turn'.[12] These were useful notions, but they obviously applied to far more of Shakespeare's plays than the three specified by Schanzer; indeed, any of Shakespeare's works may be 'problematised' by a resourceful critic. Schanzer's definition may be fruitfully applied to *Richard II*. In this play, a 'central moral problem' is that of the rebellion: is it justified or not? As for 'dramatic coquetry', it is not only Richard who divides our feelings. Consider York, apparently weak but credibly pragmatic in supporting the person who seems the most powerful. Again, Bullingbrooke initially wins some sympathy, particularly when Richard cuts off his inheritance; but gradually doubts arise: is he a covert Machiavellian? As a whole, the play provides a range of insights into politics: particularly into the contrasts between the public panoply, the outward display, and the harsher realities of the manipulations of wealth and power. It reminds us that much of what passes for recorded history is a mass of accounts of human violence, greed, exploitation and stupidity. Fallible mortals claim supernatural authority. The noted figures tend to be the powerful and prominent, rather than the considerate, kind and constructive. The play hints at the possibility that the anonymous gardener and the groom have done more good than have Richard and Bullingbrooke.

3

Richard II is usually performed on its own; but, when Shakespeare began to write it, he probably considered the possibility that it would be the first of a sequence of historical dramas dealing with a continuous phase of history. After all, his earliest endeavours at the *genre* of the history play had resulted in a tetralogy, a sequence of four works: three dealing with the reign of Henry VI and the fourth portraying the subsequent reign of Richard III. In the event, *Richard II* was to be followed by *Henry IV, Part 1, Henry IV, Part 2*, and *Henry V*, so that another tetralogy would emerge. Then the Epilogue of *Henry V* tells us that though that Henry was a brilliant monarch, a 'star of England', he died early and was succeeded by Henry VI, whose reign was disastrous – 'Which oft our stage hath shown'. Thus, that Epilogue links the end of the second tetralogy to the beginning of the first tetralogy, creating a vast dramatic octology: a cycle of eight plays.

Within *Richard II*, there are obvious signs that Shakespeare was looking ahead to likely sequels. For instance, Harry Percy (alias 'Hotspur'), Northumberland's son, appears in Act 2, scene 3, and is introduced at some length to Bullingbrooke, whom he promises to serve loyally. Given that Hotspur has no important rôle in *Richard II*, the detailed introduction may seem superfluous; but, in the next play, *1 Henry IV*, he will figure prominently. Ironically, he will be the most valiant of the rebels against the new king. Again, before the end of *Richard II*, we hear that new ruler expressing domestic worries: in particular, his fear that his own son is proving both dissolute and disloyal:

> Can no man tell me of my unthrifty son?
> 'Tis full three months since I did see him last.
> If any plague hang over us, 'tis he.

The son in question does not appear personally in *Richard II*, but this speech serves as a prelude to *1 Henry IV*, in which we will be shown extensively the life that this son, Hal, is leading among such 'unrestrainèd loose companions' as Falstaff and Poins. Bullingbrooke remarks in *Richard II* that he perceives in Hal 'some sparks of better hope, which elder years / May happily bring forth'; and these words portend the gradual emergence, in *1* and *2 Henry IV*, of Hal as a truly valiant and noble heir to the throne, the 'better hope' being fulfilled in *Henry V*. The combination of the detailed introduction of Hotspur and the expression of paternal fears about Hal's character shows that before *Richard II* was completed, Shakespeare was already thinking ahead to a work in which much of the interest would depend on the character-contrast between two Harries: Harry Percy (Hotspur) and Harry Monmouth (Hal). In fact, Hotspur was more than twenty years older than Hal, but Shakespeare chooses to suggest that they are both youthful coevals, so as to invite us to see them in *1 Henry IV* as comparable and contrasting young rivals for power. Indeed, in that play the king even expresses the wish t'

when both were in the cradle, some fairy could have exchanged
Hotspur for his Hal. This reinforces the sense that they are equal
in years, and further establishes the network of comparisons
which helps to unite the second tetralogy.

In *Richard II*, we hear various grim prophecies that the downfall of
Richard will inevitably bring divine wrath on the head of the
usurper. Both the Bishop of Carlisle and Richard himself offer
predictions that if Bullingbrooke takes the throne, his reign will be
an era of appalling and extensive civil war. In the subsequent two
plays, we see that these prophecies are amply fulfilled. Furthermore,
their fulfilment is systematically emphasised by Shakespeare. In Act
5, scene 1, of *Richard II*, Richard tells the Earl of Northumberland:

> Northumberland, thou ladder wherewithal
> The mounting Bullingbrooke ascends my throne,
> The time shall not be many hours of age
> More than it is, ere foul sin, gathering head,
> Shall break into corruption. Thou shalt think,
> Though he divide the realm and give thee half,
> It is too little, helping him to all.

In *1 Henry IV*, the prophecy is vindicated: we see that Northumberland, who had helped Bullingbrooke to power, is now
conspiring against him; and, in *2 Henry IV*, as the conspiracy
continues, Bullingbrooke, now King Henry, actually quotes (very
closely if not exactly) Richard's words:

> But which of you was by –
> [*To Warwick:*] You, cousin Nevil, as I may remember –
> When Richard, with his eyes brimful of tears,
> Then checked and rated by Northumberland,
> Did speak these words, now proved a prophecy?
> 'Northumberland, thou ladder by the which
> My cousin Bullingbrooke ascends my throne' –
> Though then, God knows, I had no such intent . . .
> 'The time shall come' – thus did he follow it –
> 'The time will come, that foul sin, gathering head,
> Shall break into corruption' – so went on,
> Foretelling this same time's condition,
> And the division of our amity.[13]

Thus, any interpretation of *Richard II* should be aided by the subsequent works. Since Richard's prophecies are fulfilled, his stature is enhanced, and we may gain the impression that, though he was abundantly fallible as a man, he still had sanctity conferred on him by his office as the rightful and consecrated King of England. A related theme is inaugurated by Bullingbrooke's vow to make a penitential pilgrimage to the Holy Land. He is so beset by rebellions that he does not undertake the voyage. Near the end of *2 Henry IV*, he suffers a fatal stroke; and, dying, enquires the name of the chamber in which he was afflicted. The chamber, he is told, is called 'Jerusalem'. He responds:

> Laud be to God! Even there my life must end.
> It hath been prophesied to me, many years,
> I should not die but in Jerusalem,
> Which vainly I supposed the Holy Land.
> But bear me to that chamber; there I'll lie;
> In that Jerusalem shall Harry die.

So the reference to 'the Holy Land' in the closing lines of *Richard II* gains, with hindsight, a strongly ironic resonance.

Such connections, which are sometimes termed 'transtextualities', enrich the sequence known as the second tetralogy. A transtextuality occurs when some prominent narrative feature (e.g. a theme, a plot-sequence or a characterisation) extends across two or more literary works.[14] Identification of such a transtextuality gives an enhanced sense of the co-ordination and particularly of the ironies of the sequence under consideration. Consider, for example, the way in which the theme of 'the sleepless monarch' is sounded. Although apoplexy may be the immediate cause of Henry's death, *2 Henry IV* gives the impression that he is driven to death mainly by sheer weariness induced by the cares of state, and in particular by his worries as he contends with rebellion after rebellion. As the rebels point out, it was he who set their example: in usurping the throne of a king, he has created a precedent for others. (Richard's true heir was Edmund Mortimer.[15]) Henry IV endures sleepless nights, envying the slumbers enjoyed by humble subjects. In a speech which sheds light on his earlier motives, he confesses to his son that

God knows . . .
By what by-paths and indirect crook'd ways
I met this crown, and I myself know well
How troublesome it sat upon my head.

In *Henry V*, we see that that son, too, is a sleepless worried
monarch who envies the slumbers of the humble. In both plays,
the wakefulness induced by cares of state is linked to guilt at the
deposition of Richard. Henry V may seem to be a splendidly
successful monarch, uniting Scots, Irish, Welsh and English
beneath his banner when he goes abroad to fight the French; but,
on the eve of the Battle of Agincourt, after walking among the
troops, he reflects bitterly on the guilt he has inherited with the
ill-gotten throne:

Not today, O Lord,
O not today, think not upon the fault
My father made in compassing the crown!
I Richard's body have interrèd new,
And on it have bestowed more contrite tears
Than from it issued forcèd drops of blood.
Five hundred poor I have in yearly pay,
Who twice a year their withered hands hold up
Toward heaven, to pardon blood; and I have built
Two chantries, where the sad and solemn priests
Sing still for Richard's soul. More will I do,
Though all that I can do is nothing worth,
Since that my penitence comes after all,
Imploring pardon.

In the event, it appears that God does, at last, decide to grant that
pardon. At the Battle of Agincourt, the English army gains an
apparently miraculous victory over the far more numerous
French forces. 'O God, thy arm was here', says the grateful Henry
V. But a long and bloody era has preceded the successful
outcome. Richard has cast a long and ominous shadow over the
usurpers. It could be said, indeed, that Shakespeare's story of
Richard is not completed until Act 5 of *Henry V*; and perhaps not
even then. (The Christian paradox of the Fortunate Fall is
distantly recalled in this second tetralogy. The Fall of Man was

bad but led to good. The rebellion against Richard was bad and provoked wrath; but in the long term it was also good, for it led to the eventual successes of Henry V.) Devout Christians, particularly if they are English rather than French, may feel that Shakespeare is emphasising the truth, which is that a good God presides over historical processes. Sceptics, in contrast, may feel that Shakespeare, reflecting the values of his times, is providing a patriotic falsification of history by suggesting that English political ambitions are fulfilling a supernatural master-plan. Nevertheless, that Chorus which concludes *Henry V* should be remembered:

> Henry the Sixth, in infant bands crowned King
> Of France and England, did this King succeed:
> Whose state so many hand the managing,
> That they lost France and made his England bleed:
> Which oft our stage hath shown . . .

The apparently triumphant closure near the end of *Henry V* is thus subverted rather than qualified. This final Chorus undermines that sense of a progressive evolution from the age of Richard II; and it introduces a daunting suggestion that history is cyclical: after civil war, civil peace, but then civil war again; and, after usurpation, orderly succession, but then further usurpation. These eight plays (from *1 Henry VI* to *Henry V*) certainly helped to generate a sense of English national identity, and some of their great patriotic speeches resonate to this day; but they also testify to the appalling cost in human lives exacted over the centuries by political ambition and ideological intolerance.

The Chorus which opens Act 5 of *Henry V* praises explicitly the Earl of Essex, who was a friend and relative of Shakespeare's patron, the Earl of Southampton. In February 1601, Essex, supported by Southampton, rebelled against Queen Elizabeth. The venture failed: Essex was executed, and Southampton (sentenced to death, but spared,) was jailed. It is well known that Essex's supporters paid Shakespeare's company to stage a special performance of *Richard II* on the eve of the rebellion.[16] Clearly, the conspirators believed that the staged spectacle of a successful uprising against a monarch would provide an inspiring prelude. The earliest printed texts of the play lack the deposition scene, which was evidently censored. Elizabeth is reported to have remarked angrily, 'I am Richard II[:]

know ye not that?'.[17] Shakespeare's play may have dealt with events of the fourteenth century; but it was also contemporaneous in reference, dealing with the real fears and ambitions of his day. If Essex's supporters had given attention to those historical plays which followed *Richard II*, they might have been deterred from risking (and, in some cases, losing) their lives. *Richard II* is a brilliant fictional history with a tentacular grip on sombre historical realities.

NOTES TO THE INTRODUCTION:

1   Thus King Edward II, responding to a command by the Earl of Leicester, in *Edward II* (reprinted by Steane as *Edward the Second*). See Christopher Marlowe: *The Complete Plays*, ed. J. B. Steane (Harmondsworth: Penguin, 1969; rpt., 1978), p. 506.

2   I preserve the First Quarto's inconsistent capitalisation.

3   *The Works of Geoffrey Chaucer*, ed. F. N. Robinson (2nd edn.: London: Oxford University Press, 1957), p. 189. A. C. Bradley: *Shakespearean Tragedy* (London: Macmillan, 1904; rpt., 1957), p. 28.

4   *Narrative and Dramatic Sources of Shakespeare*, Vol. III, ed. Geoffrey Bullough (London: Routledge & Kegan Paul, 1960; rpt., 1966), pp. 356–7. I preserve Bullough's inconsistent capitalisation of 'King'.

5   Christopher Marlowe: *The Complete Plays*, pp. 509–10. I add the two grave accents.

6   Shakespeare also recalled Holinshed's account of Richard's bounty in providing food and drink for 'ten thousand persons' daily at his court. See Raphael Holinshed et al.: *Chronicles*, Vol. III (London, 1587), p. 508.

7   Margaret Wade Labarge, in *Henry V* (London: Secker & Warburg, 1975, p. 6), says that Isabella was six at the time of the wedding. Anthony Steel's *Richard II* (London: Cambridge University Press, 1941; rpt., 1962; p. 213), says 'not yet eight'. Other historians say 'seven'. (A second ceremony took place on 1 November 1396.) Incidentally, at the time of Bullingbrooke's marriage, Bullingbrooke was 'perhaps fourteen or fifteen' and his bride, Mary, 'only ten or eleven'. She produced a child in the following year. Henry of Monmouth (later Henry V) was born when Mary was seventeen. (Labarge, pp. 1–2.)

8   A. R. Myers: *England in the Late Middle Ages* (Harmondsworth: Penguin, 1952; rpt., 1956), pp. 13–15. Quotation: Sydney Armitage-Smith: *John of Gaunt* (London: Constable, 1904; rpt., 1964), p. 281. Savoy: Armitage-Smith, pp. 246–9.

9   See 'Who Killed Woodstock?' in John Sutherland and Cedric Watts: *Henry V, War Criminal? and Other Shakespeare Puzzles* (Oxford: Oxford University Press, 2000), pp. 92–8; and Myers, p. 17.

10 Steel, pp. 267–8. Harold F. Hutchison: *The Hollow Crown* (London: Eyre and Spottiswoode, 1961), p.221.

11 See *Chronicles of the Revolution: 1397–1400: The Reign of Richard II*, translated and edited by Chris Given-Wilson (Manchester and New York: Manchester University Press, 1993), pp. 50–51; and Steel, pp. 286–7. In view of the ruthlessness of the historic Bullingbrooke's ascent to power, and given that Richard, while alive, remained a focus of possible rebellions against the new king, I think it probable that Richard was deliberately starved: a method of murder which would leave no signs of violence. Different historians make diverse claims, and there is no certainty.

12 Ernest Schanzer: *The Problem Plays of Shakespeare: A Study of 'Julius Caesar', 'Measure for Measure' and 'Antony and Cleopatra'* (London: Routledge & Kegan Paul, 1963; rpt., 1965), pp. 6 and 70.

13 A transtextuality is quite different from 'intertextuality', which Julia Kristeva has defined as the vast sum of cultural knowledge which makes it possible for texts to have meaning and which causes every text, including her own, to be merely 'a mosaic of quotations' (see her *Semeiotike*: Paris: du Seuil, 1969; p. 146). Intertextuality dissolves the sense of authorial integrity; transtextuality restores it. See Cedric Watts: *The Deceptive Text: An Introduction to Covert Plots* (Brighton: Harvester, 1984).

14 The fact that the quotation from the earlier play is reasonably close but not exact suggests that Shakespeare did not consult his own previous writing but relied on a very good (if imperfect) memory, as an actor would.

15 At the time of Richard's death, Edmund Mortimer was eight years old. Later, as the Holinshed *Chronicle* reports (Vol. III, pp. 548–9), Henry V executed the Earl of Cambridge, who was said to have conspired on behalf of Edmund (his brother-in-law).

16 Other playwrights had depicted Richard II, but, as Charles Forker states, the current 'general consensus' is that the play performed was Shakespeare's. (After all, the playwright was well known to the ringleaders.) See Charles R. Forker: *Shakespeare: The Critical Tradition: 'Richard II'* (London and Atlantic Highlands, N.J.: Athlone Press, 1998), p. 56.

17 She is quoted in *The Progresses and Public Processions of Queen Elizabeth*, Vol. III, ed. John Nichols (New York: Franklin, n.d.), p. 552. Her court favourites were known as 'Richard II's men'.

FURTHER READING
(in chronological order)

E. M. W. Tillyard: *Shakespeare's History Plays*. London: Chatto and Windus, 1944; reprinted, Harmondsworth: Penguin, 1962.

Derek Traversi: *Shakespeare from 'Richard II' to 'Henry V'*. London: Hollis & Carter, 1958; rpt., 1968.

Narrative and Dramatic Sources of Shakespeare, Vol. III, ed. Geoffrey Bullough. London: Routledge & Kegan Paul; New York: Columbia University Press, 1960; rpt., 1966.

William Shakespeare: *Richard the Second 1597* (Shakespeare Quarto Facsimiles, No. 13). London: Oxford University Press, 1966.

Samuel Schoenbaum: *William Shakespeare: A Compact Documentary Life*. London and New York: Oxford University Press, 1977; rpt., 1987.

Graham Holderness: *Shakespeare's History*. Dublin: Gill and Macmillan, 1985.

Political Shakespeare: New Essays in Cultural Materialism, ed. Jonathan Dollimore and Alan Sinfield. Manchester: Manchester University Press, 1985.

Robin Headlam Wells: *Shakespeare, Politics and the State*. Basingstoke: Macmillan, 1986.

Leonard Tennenhouse: *Power on Display: The Politics of Shakespeare's Genres*. London and New York: Methuen, 1986.

C. W. R. D. Moseley: *Shakespeare's History Plays: Richard II to Henry V: The Making of a King*. London: Penguin, 1988.

Critical Essays on 'Richard II', ed. Linda Cookson and Bryan Loughrey. Harlow: Longman, 1989.

Graham Holderness: *William Shakespeare: 'Richard II'*. London: Penguin, 1989.

Brian Vickers: *Appropriating Shakespeare: Contemporary Critical Quarrels*. New Haven and London: Yale University Press, 1993.

Jean E. Howard and Phyllis Rackin: *Engendering a Nation: A Feminist Account of Shakespeare's English Histories*. London and New York: Routledge, 1997.

Margaret Healy: *William Shakespeare: Richard II*. Plymouth: Northcote House, 1998.

Shakespeare: The Critical Tradition: Richard II, ed. Charles R. Forker. London and Atlantic Highlands, N.J.: Athlone Press, 1998.

A Companion to Shakespeare, ed. David Scott Kastan. Oxford: Blackwell, 1999.

John Sutherland and Cedric Watts: *Henry V, War Criminal? and Other Shakespeare Puzzles*. Oxford: Oxford University Press, 2000.

James R. Siemon: *Word against Word: Shakespearean Utterance*. Amherst and Boston: University of Massachusetts Press, 2002.

Shakespeare: An Oxford Guide, ed. Stanley Wells and Lena Cowen Orlin. Oxford: Oxford University Press, 2003.

Andrew Hadfield: *Shakespeare and Republicanism*. Cambridge: Cambridge University Press, 2005.

'Introduction': William Shakespeare: *Richard II*, ed. Anthony B. Dawson and Paul Yachnin. Oxford: Oxford University Press, 2011.

NOTE ON SHAKESPEARE

William Shakespeare was the son of a glover at Stratford-upon-Avon, and tradition gives his date of birth as 23 April, 1564; certainly, three days later, he was christened at the parish church. It is likely that he attended the local Grammar School but had no university education. Of his early career there is no record, though John Aubrey reports a claim that he was a rural schoolmaster. In 1582 Shakespeare married Anne Hathaway, with whom he had two daughters, Susanna and Judith, and a son, Hamnet, who died in 1596. How he became involved with the stage in London is uncertain, but by 1592 he was sufficiently established as a playwright to be criticised in print as a challengingly versatile 'upstart Crow'. He was a leading member of the Lord Chamberlain's company, which became the King's Men on the accession of James I in 1603. The players performed at a wide variety of locations. Being not only a playwright and an actor but also a 'sharer' (one of the owners of the company, entitled to a share of the profits), Shakespeare prospered greatly, as is proven by the numerous records of his financial transactions. Meanwhile, his sonnets expressed the poet's love for a beautiful young man and a 'dark lady'. Towards the end of his life, Shakespeare loosened his ties with London and retired to New Place, the large house in Stratford-upon-Avon which he had bought in 1597. He died on 23 April, 1616, and is buried in the place of his baptism, Holy Trinity Church. The earliest edition of his collected plays, the First Folio, was published in 1623, and its prefatory verse-tributes include Ben Jonson's famous declaration, 'He was not of an age, but for all time'.

ACKNOWLEDGEMENTS AND
TEXTUAL MATTERS

I have consulted – and am indebted to – numerous editions of *Richard II*, notably those by: John Dover Wilson (London: Cambridge University Press, 1939; rpt., 1961; and abridged edition, 1957); Peter Alexander (London and Glasgow: Collins, 1951; rpt., 1966); Peter Ure ('The Arden Shakespeare': London: Methuen, 1956; rpt., 1966); Kenneth Muir ('The Signet Classic Shakespeare': New York and London: New English Library, 1963); G. Blakemore Evans *et al.* (*The Riverside Shakespeare*: Boston, Mass.: Houghton Mifflin, 1974); Andrew Gurr ('The New Cambridge Shakespeare': Cambridge: Cambridge University Press, 1985; updated edition, 2003); Stanley Wells and Gary Taylor (*The Complete Works: Compact Edition*: Oxford: Oxford University Press, 1988); Stephen Greenblatt *et al.* (*The Norton Shakespeare*: New York and London: Norton, 1997); Charles R. Forker ('The Arden Shakespeare': London: Thomson Learning, 2002); and Anthony B. Dawson and Paul Yachnin ('Oxford World's Classics': Oxford University Press, 2011). The Glossary radically revises Dover Wilson's. To Antony Gray, who has been responsible for the typesetting of seventeen of my Shakespeare editions, I express my gratitude for his patience and skill.

Richard II was written in or around 1595 and was probably performed in that year. It was registered in 1597, and the First Quarto (Q1) appeared in 1597. (A 'quarto' is a book with relatively small pages, each leaf having been folded twice, while a 'folio' is a book with relatively large pages, each leaf having been folded once.) Other quartos, Q2 and Q3, were published in 1598. Then Q4 (1608, followed by Q5 in 1615) restored the crucial sequence of deposition and abdication, which had been absent from the previous texts. In the present edition, that sequence extends inclusively from line 154 to line 318 of Act IV, scene 1. In 1623 appeared the First Folio (F1), the first edition of Shakespeare's collected works, assembled after the playwright's death by two of his former colleagues, John Heminge (or Heminges) and Henry Condell. The First Quarto text of *Richard II* appears to derive from Shakespeare's 'foul papers' (an untidy manuscript), and, fo

editorial purposes, is of reasonably good quality, though it lacks
that abdication sequence. The text in the First Folio is also
generally good, frequently improving the punctuation and
the metre; but, while it includes a better version of Richard's
abdication than did Q4 and Q5, it elsewhere lacks various passages
which were present in Q1 and later quartos.

Numerous scholars believe that the sequence of deposition
and abdication was omitted from the early texts as a result of
censorship. There is an alternative belief that Shakespeare wrote
that part of the work later, in the early years of the seventeenth
century. My view is that censorship was indeed responsible for the
shorter text, but the full scene was probably performed from the
play's inception. Holinshed's account of Richard's deposition was
present in the first edition of his *Chronicles* in 1577 but was cut from
the second in 1587; and Queen Elizabeth's political distaste for the
play is well known.

The present Wordsworth edition of *Richard II* offers a practical
compromise between the early texts, Shakespeare's intentions
(insofar as they can be reasonably inferred) and modern require-
ments. In the interest of fidelity to Shakespeare's likely usages and
euphonies, I have retained various archaisms which most other
editions modernise: for instance, 'Bullingbrooke' (instead of
'Bolingbroke'), 'Bristow' ('Bristol') and 'Callice' ('Calais'). The
glossary explains archaic and unfamiliar terms, while the
annotations offer clarification of obscurities. No edition of the
play can claim to be definitive, but this one – aiming at clarity and
concise practicality – can promise to be very useful.

THE TRAGEDY OF KING RICHARD THE SECOND

CHARACTERS:

KING RICHARD II.

QUEEN ISABELLA, *his wife.*

JOHN OF GAUNT, *Duke of Lancaster, Richard's uncle.*

HENRY BULLINGBROOKE, *Duke of Hereford, Gaunt's son.*

The DUCHESS OF GLOUCESTER, *widow of Gaunt's brother,*
    Thomas Woodstock, Duke of Gloucester.

The DUKE OF YORK, *Richard's uncle.*

The DUCHESS OF YORK.

The DUKE OF AUMERLE, *Earl of Rutland, their son.*

THOMAS MOWBRAY, *Duke of Norfolk.*

BUSHY, BAGOT *and* GREENE, *followers of Richard.*

NORTHUMBERLAND *(Henry Percy, Earl of Northumberland).*

HENRY (HARRY) PERCY, *his son, later known as Hotspur.*

LORDS ROSS, WILLOUGHBY, FITZWATER *and* BERKELEY.

The DUKE OF SURREY.

The BISHOP OF CARLISLE.

The ABBOT OF WESTMINSTER.

SIR STEPHEN SCROOPE.

SIR PIERCE OF EXTON.

The LORD MARSHAL.

A CAPTAIN *of Welsh soldiers.*

A GARDENER.

A KEEPER.

A GROOM.

LORDS, LADIES, OFFICERS, SOLDIERS, GUARDS,
HERALDS, ATTENDANTS *and* SERVANTS.

Locations: England; Wales; England again.

RICHARD II[1]

ACT I, SCENE I.

Windsor. Open ground inside the castle, with seating for spectators of a combat.

Enter KING RICHARD, JOHN OF GAUNT, *the* DUKE OF SURREY *(the Lord Marshal), other* NOBLEMEN *and* ATTENDANTS.

RICHARD   Old John of Gaunt, time-honoured Lancaster,
Hast thou, according to thy oath and band,
Brought hither Henry Her'ford, thy bold son,
Here to make good the boist'rous late appeal,
Which then our leisure would not let us hear,
Against the Duke of Norfolk, Thomas Mowbray?

GAUNT   I have, my liege.

RICHARD   Tell me, moreover, hast thou sounded him,
If he appeal the Duke on ancient malice,
Or worthily, as a good subject should,   10
On some known ground of treachery in him?

GAUNT   As near as I could sift him on that argument,
On some apparent danger seen in him
Aimed at your Highness; no inveterate malice.

RICHARD   Then call them to our presence. [*Exit attendant.*]
                           Face to face,
And frowning brow to brow, ourselves will hear
The accuser and the accusèd freely speak:
High-stomached are they both and full of ire,
In rage, deaf as the sea, hasty as fire.

Enter BULLINGBROOKE *(Duke of Hereford) and*
MOWBRAY *(Duke of Norfolk)*

BULLING.   Many years of happy days befall   20
My gracious Sovereign, my most loving liege!

MOWBRAY   Each day still better other's happiness,
Until the heavens, envying earth's good hap,
Add an immortal title to your crown!

RICHARD   We thank you both; yet one but flatters us,
As well appeareth by the cause you come,

Namely, to appeal each other of high treason.
Cousin of Her'ford, what dost thou object
Against the Duke of Norfolk, Thomas Mowbray?

BULLING. First (heaven be the record to my speech),   30
In the devotion of a subject's love,
Tend'ring the precious safety of my Prince,
And free from other misbegotten hate,
Come I appellant to this princely presence.
– Now, Thomas Mowbray, do I turn to thee;
And mark my greeting well: for what I speak,
My body shall make good upon this earth,
Or my divine soul answer it in heaven:
Thou art a traitor and a miscreant,
Too good to be so,² and too bad to live,   40
Since the more fair and crystal is the sky,
The uglier seem the clouds that in it fly.
Once more, the more to aggravate the note,
With a foul traitor's name stuff I thy throat,
And wish (so please my Sovereign) ere I move,
What my tongue speaks, my right drawn sword may
                                    prove.

MOWBRAY Let not my cold words here accuse my zeal:
'Tis not the trial of a woman's war,
The bitter clamour of two eager tongues,
Can arbitrate this cause betwixt us twain: 50
The blood is hot that must be cooled for this.
Yet can I not of such tame patience boast
As to be hushed and nought at all to say.
First, the fair reverence of your Highness curbs me
From giving reins and spurs to my free speech,
Which else would post until it had returned
These terms of treason doubled down his throat.
Setting aside his high blood's royalty,
And let him be no kinsman to my liege,
I do defy him, and I spit at him,   60
Call him a slanderous coward, and a villain,
Which to maintain, I would allow him odds,
And meet him were I tied to run afoot
Even to the frozen ridges of the Alps,

Or any other ground inhabitable,
Where ever Englishman durst set his foot.
Mean time, let this defend my loyalty –
By all my hopes, most falsely doth he lie.[3]

BULLING.   [throwing down his gage:[4]] Pale trembling coward, there
                                                    I throw my gage,
Disclaiming here the kindred of the King,
And lay aside my high blood's royalty,   70
Which fear, not reverence, makes thee to except.
If guilty dread have left thee so much strength
As to take up mine honour's pawn, then stoop.
By that, and all the rites of knighthood else,
Will I make good against thee, arm to arm,
What I have spoke, or thou canst worse devise.

MOWBRAY   [picking up the gage:] I take it up, and by that sword
                                                    I swear,
Which gently laid my knighthood on my shoulder,
I'll answer thee in any fair degree,   80
Or chivalrous design of knightly trial;
And when I mount, alive may I not light,
If I be traitor or unjustly fight!

RICHARD   What doth our cousin lay to Mowbray's charge?
It must be great that can inherit us
So much as of a thought of ill in him.

BULLING.   Look what I speak, my life shall prove it true:
That Mowbray hath received eight thousand nobles
In name of lendings for your Highness' soldiers,
The which he hath detained for lewd employments,   90
Like a false traitor and injurious villain;
Besides I say, and will in battle prove,
Or here, or elsewhere to the furthest verge
That ever was surveyed by English eye,
That all the treasons for these eighteen years[5]
Complotted and contrivèd in this land
Fetch from false Mowbray their first head and spring.
Further I say, and further will maintain
Upon his bad life to make all this good,
That he did plot the Duke of Gloucester's death,
Suggest his soon-believing adversaries,

And consequently, like a traitor coward,
Sluiced out his innocent soul through streams of blood,
Which blood, like sacrificing Abel's, cries,
Even from the tongueless caverns of the earth,
To me for justice and rough chastisement;
And, by the glorious worth of my descent,
This arm shall do it, or this life be spent.[6]

RICHARD   How high a pitch his resolution soars!
Thomas of Norfolk, what say'st thou to this?   110

MOWBRAY   O let my sovereign turn away his face
And bid his ears a little while be deaf,
Till I have told this slander of his blood
How God and good men hate so foul a liar.

RICHARD   Mowbray, impartial are our eyes and ears.
Were he my brother, nay, my kingdom's heir,
As he is but my father's brother's son,
Now, by my sceptre's awe, I make a vow,
Such neighbour-nearness to our sacred blood
Should nothing privilege him nor partialize   120
The unstooping firmness of my upright soul.
He is our subject, Mowbray; so art thou;
Free speech and fearless I to thee allow.

MOWBRAY   Then, Bullingbrooke, as low as to thy heart
Through the false passage of thy throat, thou liest!
Three parts of that receipt I had for Callice
Disbursed I duly to his Highness' soldiers;
The other part reserved I by consent,
For that my sovereign liege was in my debt
Upon remainder of a dear account[7]   130
Since last I went to France to fetch his Queen:
Now swallow down that lie. For Gloucester's death:
I slew him not, but (to my own disgrace)
Neglected my sworn duty in that case.
– For you, my noble lord of Lancaster,
The honourable father to my foe:
Once did I lay an ambush for your life,
A trespass that doth vex my grièved soul;
But ere I last received the Sacrament,
I did confess it, and exactly begged   140

          Your Grace's pardon, and I hope I had it.[8]
          This is my fault. As for the rest appealed,
          It issues from the rancour of a villain,
          A recreant and most degenerate traitor;
          Which in myself I boldly will defend,
          And interchangeably hurl down my gage
          Upon this overweening traitor's foot,   [*He hurls it.*]
          To prove myself a loyal gentleman,
          Even in the best blood chambered in his bosom.
          In haste whereof, most heartily I pray   150
          Your Highness to assign our trial day.
                     [*Bullingbrooke picks up the gage.*

RICHARD   Wrath-kindled gentlemen, be ruled by me:
          Let's purge this choler without letting blood.[9]
          This we prescribe, though no physician;
          Deep malice makes too deep incision.
          Forget, forgive, conclude and be agreed;
          Our doctors say this is no month to bleed.
          – Good uncle, let this end where it begun:
          We'll calm the Duke of Norfolk, you your son.

GAUNT   To be a make-peace shall become my age.   160
          – Throw down, my son, the Duke of Norfolk's gage.

RICHARD   And, Norfolk, throw down his.

GAUNT   When, Harry? When?
          Obedience bids I should not bid again.

RICHARD   Norfolk, throw down, we bid; there is no boot.

MOWBRAY [*kneeling:*] Myself I throw, dread Sovereign, at thy foot.
          My life thou shalt command, but not my shame:
          The one my duty owes; but my fair name,
          Despite of death that lives upon my grave,
          To dark dishonour's use thou shalt not have.
          I am disgraced, impeached, and baffled here,   170
          Pierced to the soul with slander's venomed spear,
          The which no balm can cure but his heart-blood
          Which breathed this poison.[10]

RICHARD   Rage must be withstood:
          Give me his gage; lions make leopards tame.

MOWBRAY Yea, but not change his spots: take but my shame,
          And I resign my gage.[11] My dear dear lord,

The purest treasure mortal times afford
Is spotless reputation: that away,
Men are but gilded loam or painted clay.
A jewel in a ten-times barred-up chest   180
Is a bold spirit in a loyal breast.
Mine honour is my life; both grow in one:
Take honour from me, and my life is done.
Then, dear my liege, mine honour let me try:
In that I live, and for that will I die.   [*He stands.*

RICHARD   – Cousin, throw up your gage: do you begin!

BULLING.   O God defend my soul from such deep sin!
Shall I seem crest-fall'n in my father's sight,
Or with pale beggar-fear impeach my height
Before this out-dared dastard? Ere my tongue   190
Shall wound my honour with such feeble wrong,
Or sound so base a parle, my teeth shall tear
The slavish motive of recanting fear,
And spit it bleeding in his high disgrace,
Where shame doth harbour, even in Mowbray's face.

RICHARD   We were not born to sue, but to command;
Which since we cannot do to make you friends,
Be ready (as your lives shall answer it)
At Coventry upon Saint Lambert's Day.
There shall your swords and lances arbitrate   200
The swelling difference of your settled hate.
Since we can not atone you, we shall see
Justice design the victor's chivalry.[12]
Lord Marshal, command our officers-at-arms
Be ready to direct these home alarms.   [*Exeunt.*

SCENE 2.

Inside the house of John of Gaunt (Duke of Lancaster).

Enter JOHN OF GAUNT *with the*
DUCHESS OF GLOUCESTER *(Woodstock's widow).*

GAUNT   Alas, the part I had in Woodstock's blood[13]
Doth more solicit me than your exclaims
To stir against the butchers of his life;

           But since correction lieth in those hands
           Which made the fault that we cannot correct,
           Put we our quarrel to the will of heaven,
           Who, when they see the hours ripe on earth,[14]
           Will rain hot vengeance on offenders' heads.

DUCHESS   Finds brotherhood in thee no sharper spur?
           Hath love in thy old blood no living fire?   10
           Edward's seven sons, whereof thyself art one,
           Were as seven vials of his sacred blood,
           Or seven fair branches springing from one root:
           Some of those seven are dried by nature's course,
           Some of those branches by the Destinies cut;
           But Thomas, my dear lord, my life, my Gloucester,
           One vial full of Edward's sacred blood,
           One flourishing branch of his most royal root,
           Is cracked, and all the precious liquor spilt,
           Is hacked down, and his summer leaves all faded,   20
           By envy's hand, and murder's bloody axe.
           Ah Gaunt, his blood was thine. That bed, that womb,
           That mettle, that self mould, that fashioned thee,
           Made him a man; and though thou liv'st and breathest,
           Yet art thou slain in him. Thou dost consent
           In some large measure to thy father's death,
           In that thou seest thy wretched brother die,
           Who was the model of thy father's life.
           Call it not patience, Gaunt; it is despair.
           In suff'ring thus thy brother to be slaughtered,   30
           Thou show'st the naked pathway to thy life,
           Teaching stern murder how to butcher thee.
           That which in mean men we entitle patience
           Is pale cold cowardice in noble breasts.
           What shall I say? To safeguard thine own life,
           The best way is to venge my Gloucester's death.

GAUNT   God's is the quarrel; for God's substitute,
           His deputy anointed in His sight,
           Hath caused his death, the which if wrongfully,
           Let heaven revenge, for I may never lift
           An angry arm against His minister.

DUCHESS   Where then, alas, may I complain myself?

GAUNT To God, the widow's champion and defence.
DUCHESS Why then, I will. Farewell, old Gaunt.
     Thou goest to Coventry, there to behold
     Our cousin Her'ford and fell Mowbray fight.
     O set my husband's wrongs on Her'ford's spear,
     That it may enter butcher Mowbray's breast!
     Or if misfortune miss the first career,
     Be Mowbray's sins so heavy in his bosom   50
     That they may break his foaming courser's back
     And throw the rider headlong in the lists,
     A caitiff recreant to my cousin Her'ford!
     Farewell, old Gaunt: thy sometimes brother's wife
     With her companion, Grief, must end her life.
GAUNT Sister, farewell; I must to Coventry.
     As much good stay with thee, as go with me.
DUCHESS Yet one word more. Grief boundeth where it falls,
     Not with the empty hollowness, but weight.
     I take my leave before I have begun,   60
     For sorrow ends not when it seemeth done.
     Commend me to thy brother, Edmund York.
     Lo, this is all. Nay, yet depart not so;
     Though this be all, do not so quickly go;
     I shall remember more. Bid him – ah what? –
     With all good speed at Plashie visit me.
     Alack, and what shall good old York there see
     But empty lodgings and unfurnished walls,
     Unpeopled offices, untrodden stones?
     And what hear there for welcome but my groans? 70
     Therefore commend me; let him not come there
     To seek out sorrow that dwells everywhere.
     Desolate, desolate, will I hence and die:
     The last leave of thee takes my weeping eye.
            [*Exeunt separately.*

SCENE 3.

Coventry. The lists (tournament-area).

Enter the LORD MARSHAL, *the* DUKE OF AUMERLE
and OFFICERS.

MARSHAL   My Lord Aumerle, is Harry Her'ford armed?
AUMERLE   Yea, at all points, and longs to enter in.
MARSHAL   The Duke of Norfolk, sprightfully and bold,
          Stays but the summons of the appellant's trumpet.
AUMERLE   Why then the champions are prepared, and stay
          For nothing but his Majesty's approach.

Trumpets sound. Enter the KING *(bearing a baton), and* NOBLEMEN,
including GAUNT, BUSHY, BAGOT *and* GREENE. *When they are seated,
enter* MOWBRAY *in armour as defendant.*

RICHARD   Marshal, demand of yonder champion
          The cause of his arrival here in arms.
          Ask him his name, and orderly proceed
          To swear him in the justice of his cause.   10
MARSHAL   In God's name and the King's, say who thou art,
          And why thou com'st thus knightly clad in arms,
          Against what man thou com'st, and what thy quarrel.
          Speak truly, on thy knighthood and thy oath,
          And so defend thee heaven and thy valour!
MOWBRAY My name is Thomas Mowbray, Duke of Norfolk,
          Who hither come engagèd by my oath
          (Which God defend a knight should violate!)
          Both to defend my loyalty and truth
          To God, my King, and my succeeding issue,   20
          Against the Duke of Her'ford that appeals me,
          And by the grace of God, and this mine arm,
          To prove him, in defending of myself,
          A traitor to my God, my King, and me.
          And as I truly fight, defend me heaven!

Trumpets sound. Enter BULLINGBROOKE *in armour as appellant.*

RICHARD   Marshal, ask yonder knight in arms
          Both who he is, and why he cometh hither,

Thus plated in habiliments of war;
And formally, according to our law,
Depose him in the justice of his cause.   30

MARSHAL What is thy name? And wherefore com'st thou hither
Before King Richard in his royal lists?
Against whom comest thou? And what's thy quarrel?
Speak like a true knight, so defend thee heaven!

BULLING. Harry of Her'ford, Lancaster and Derby
Am I, who ready here do stand in arms
To prove by God's grace, and my body's valour
In lists, on Thomas Mowbray, Duke of Norfolk,
That he's a traitor, foul and dangerous,
To God of heaven, King Richard, and to me;   40
And as I truly fight, defend me heaven!

MARSHAL On pain of death, no person be so bold
Or daring-hardy as to touch the lists,
Except the Marshal and such officers
Appointed to direct these fair designs.

BULLING. Lord Marshal, let me kiss my Sovereign's hand,
And bow my knee before his Majesty;
For Mowbray and myself are like two men
That vow a long and weary pilgrimage:
Then let us take a ceremonious leave,   50
And loving fárewell of our several friends.

MARSHAL The appellant in all duty greets your Highness,
And craves to kiss your hand, and take his leave.

RICHARD [rising:] We will descend and fold him in our arms.
                    [He descends and embraces Bullingbrooke.
Cousin of Her'ford, as thy cause is right,
So be thy fortune in this royal fight.
Farewell, my blood, which if today thou shed,
Lament we may, but not revenge thee dead.

BULLING. O, let no noble eye profane a tear
For me, if I be gored with Mowbray's spear.   60
As confident as is the falcon's flight
Against a bird, do I with Mowbray fight.
[To Marshal:] My loving lord, I take my leave of you;
[To Aumerle:] Of you (my noble cousin), Lord Aumerle;
Not sick, although I have to do with death,

But lusty, young, and cheerly drawing breath.
[*To Gaunt:*] Lo, as at English feasts, so I regreet
The daintiest last, to make the end most sweet.
O thou, the earthly author of my blood,
Whose youthful sprite, in me regenerate,   70
Doth with a twofold vigour lift me up
To reach at victory above my head,
Add proof unto mine armour with thy prayers,
And with thy blessings steel my lance's point
That it may enter Mowbray's waxen coat
And furbish new the name of John a Gaunt,
Even in the lusty haviour of his son.

GAUNT God in thy good cause make thee prosperous:
Be swift like lightning in the execution,
And let thy blows, doubly redoublèd,   80
Fall like amazing thunder on the casque
Of thy adverse pernicious enemy!
Rouse up thy youthful blood, be valiant and live.

BULLING. Mine innocence and Saint George to thrive![15]

MOWBRAY However God or Fortune cast my lot,
There lives or dies, true to King Richard's throne,
A loyal, just, and upright gentleman.
Never did captive with a freer heart
Cast off his chains of bondage, and embrace
His golden uncontrolled enfranchisement,   90
More than my dancing soul doth celebrate
This feast of battle with mine adversary.
Most mighty liege, and my companion peers,
Take from my mouth the wish of happy years.
As gentle and as jocund as to jest
Go I to fight: truth hath a quiet breast.

RICHARD Farewell, my lord; securely I espy
Virtue with valour couchèd in thine eye.
– Order the trial, Marshal, and begin.

MARSHAL Harry of Her'ford, Lancaster and Derby,   100
Receive thy lance, and God defend the right!

BULLING. Strong as a tower in hope, I cry 'Amen'!

MARSHAL [*to an officer:*] Go bear this lance to Thomas, Duke
                                            of Norfolk.

HERALD 1   Harry of Her'ford, Lancaster and Derby,
Stands here, for God, his Sovereign and himself,
On pain to be found false and recreant,
To prove the Duke of Norfolk, Thomas Mowbray,
A traitor to his God, his King and him,
And dares him to set forward to the fight.

HERALD 2   Here standeth Thomas Mowbray, Duke of Norfolk,   110
On pain to be found false and recreant,
Both to defend himself, and to approve
Henry of Her'ford, Lancaster and Derby,
To God, his Sovereign and to him disloyal,
Courageously and with a free desire
Attending but the signal to begin.

MARSHAL   Sound trumpets; and set forward, combatants.

A charge is sounded. Before the combat can begin,
        the King throws down his baton.

Stay, the King hath thrown his warder down.

RICHARD   Let them lay by their helmets and their spears,
And both return back to their chairs again.   120

                  [Bullingbrooke and Mowbray comply.

[*To noblemen:*] Withdraw with us, and let the trumpets
                           sound
While we return these dukes what we decree.

A long flourish sounds while the King consults noblemen.
He then returns, and summons Bullingbrooke and Mowbray.

Draw near,
And list what with our council we have done.
For that our kingdom's earth should not be soiled
With that dear blood which it hath fosterèd;
And for our eyes do hate the dire aspéct
Of civil wounds ploughed up with neighbours' swords,
Which, so roused up with boist'rous untuned drums,
With harsh-resounding trumpets' dreadful bray,   130
And grating shock of wrathful iron arms,
Might from our quiet confines fright fair peace,
And make us wade even in our kindred's blood;
And for we think the eagle-wingèd pride
Of sky-aspiring and ambitious thoughts,

With rival-hating envy, set on you
To wake our peace, which in our country's cradle
Draws the sweet infant breath of gentle sleep:[16]
Therefore we banish you our territories.
You, cousin Her'ford, upon pain of life,   140
Till twice five summers have enriched our fields,
Shall not regreet our fair dominions,
But tread the stranger paths of banishment.

BULLING. Your will be done. This must my comfort be:
That sun that warms you here, shall shine on me,
And those his golden beams, to you here lent,
Shall point on me, and gild my banishment.

RICHARD Norfolk, for thee remains a heavier doom,
Which I with some unwillingness pronounce.
The sly slow hours shall not determinate   150
The dateless limit of thy dear exíle.
The hopeless word of 'never to return'
Breathe I against thee, upon pain of life.

MOWBRAY A heavy sentence, my most sovereign liege,
And all unlooked for from your Highness' mouth.
A dearer merit, not so deep a maim
As to be cast forth in the common air,
Have I deservèd at your Highness' hands.
The language I have learnt these forty years,
My native English, now I must forgo,   160
And now my tongue's use is to me no more
Than an unstringèd viol or a harp,
Or like a cunning instrument cased up,
Or, being open, put into his hands
That knows no touch to tune the harmony:
Within my mouth you have engaoled my tongue,
Doubly portcullised with my teeth and lips;
And dull unfeeling barren ignorance
Is made my gaoler to attend on me.
I am too old to fawn upon a nurse,   170
Too far in years to be a pupil now;
What is thy sentence, then, but speechless death,
Which robs my tongue from breathing native breath?

RICHARD It boots thee not to be compassionate;

After our sentence plaining comes too late.

MOWBRAY Then thus I turn me from my country's light,
To dwell in solemn shades of endless night.

                              [*He moves away.*

RICHARD Return again, and take an oath with thee.
[*To both:*] Lay on our royal sword your banished hands:
Swear by the duty that you owe to God   180
(Our part therein we banish with yourselves)[17]
To keep the oath that we administer:
You never shall, so help you truth and God,
Embrace each other's love in banishment,
Nor never look upon each other's face,
Nor never write, regreet, nor reconcile
This louring tempest of your home-bred hate,
Nor never by advisèd purpose meet
To plot, contrive or complot any ill
'Gainst us, our state, our subjects, or our land.   190

BULLING. I swear.

MOWBRAY And I, to keep all this.

BULLING. Norfolk, so fare as to mine enemy.
By this time, had the King permitted us,
One of our souls had wandered in the air,
Banished this frail sepulchre of our flesh,
As now our flesh is banished from this land.
Confess thy treasons ere thou fly the realm:
Since thou hast far to go, bear not along
The clogging burthen of a guilty soul.   200

MOWBRAY No, Bullingbrooke: if ever I were traitor,
My name be blotted from the book of life,[18]
And I from heaven banished as from hence:
But what thou art, God, thou and I do know,
And all too soon (I fear) the King shall rue.
– Farewell, my liege. Now no way can I stray:
Save back to England, all the world's my way.   [*Exit.*

RICHARD [*To Gaunt:*] Uncle, even in the glasses of thine eyes
I see thy grievèd heart. Thy sad aspèct
Hath from the number of his banished years   210
Plucked four away. [*To Bullingbrooke:*] Six frozen
                             winters spent,

	Return with welcome home from banishment.
BULLING.	How long a time lies in one little word!
	Four lagging winters and four wanton springs
	End in a word: such is the breath of kings.
GAUNT	I thank my liege that, in regard of me,
	He shortens four years of my son's exile;
	But little vantage shall I reap thereby:
	For, ere the six years that he hath to spend
	Can change their moons and bring their times about, 220
	My oil-dried lamp and time-bewasted light
	Shall be extinct with age and endless night:
	My inch of taper will be burnt and done,
	And blindfold Death not let me see my son.[19]
RICHARD	Why, uncle, thou hast many years to live.
GAUNT	But not a minute, King, that thou canst give.
	Shorten my days thou canst with sullen sorrow,
	And pluck nights from me, but not lend a morrow;
	Thou canst help Time to furrow me with age,
	But stop no wrinkle in his pilgrimage; 230
	Thy word is current with him for my death,
	But, dead, thy kingdom cannot buy my breath.
RICHARD	Thy son is banished upon good advice,
	Whereto thy tongue a party-verdict gave.
	Why at our justice seem'st thou then to lour?
GAUNT	Things sweet to taste prove in digestion sour.
	You urged me as a judge, but I had rather
	You would have bid me argue like a father.
	O, had it been a stranger, not my child,
	To smooth his fault I should have been more mild. 240
	A partial slander sought I to avoid,
	And in the sentence my own life destroyed.[20]
	Alas, I looked when some of you should say,
	I was too strict to make mine own away;
	But you gave leave to my unwilling tongue,
	Against my will to do myself this wrong.
RICHARD	– Cousin, farewell; and uncle, bid him so:
	Six years we banish him, and he shall go.

           [*Flourish. Exeunt all except Aumerle, the Marshal,*
                            Gaunt and Bullingbrooke.

AUMERLE   Cousin, farewell. What presence must not know,
          From where you do remain let paper show.[21]   250
MARSHAL   My lord, no leave take I, for I will ride
          As far as land will let me by your side.
GAUNT   O, to what purpose dost thou hoard thy words,
          That thou return'st no greeting to thy friends?
BULLING. I have too few to take my leave of you,
          When the tongue's office should be prodigal
          To breathe the abundant dolour of the heart.
GAUNT   Thy grief is but thy absence for a time.
BULLING. Joy absent, grief is present for that time.
GAUNT   What is six winters? They are quickly gone –   260
BULLING. To men in joy; but grief makes one hour ten.
GAUNT   Call it a travel that thou tak'st for pleasure.
BULLING. My heart will sigh when I miscall it so,
          Which finds it an enforcèd pilgrimage.
GAUNT   The sullen passage of thy weary steps
          Esteem as foil wherein thou art to set
          The precious jewel of thy home return.
BULLING. Nay, rather, every tedious stride I make
          Will but remember me what a deal of world
          I wander from the jewels that I love.   270
          Must I not serve a long apprenticehood
          To foreign passages, and, in the end,
          Having my freedom, boast of nothing else
          But that I was a journeyman to grief?
GAUNT   All places that the eye of heaven visits
          Are to a wise man ports and happy havens.
          Teach thy necessity to reason thus;
          There is no virtue like necessity.
          Think not the King did banish thee,
          But thou the King. Woe doth the heavier sit,   280
          Where it perceives it is but faintly borne.
          Go, say I sent thee forth to purchase honour,
          And not the King exíled thee; or suppose
          Devouring pestilence hangs in our air,
          And thou art flying to a fresher clime.
          Look, what thy soul holds dear, imagine it
          To lie that way thou goest, not whence thou com'st:

        Suppose the singing birds musicians,
        The grass whereon thou tread'st the presence strewed,
        The flowers fair ladies, and thy steps no more   290
        Than a delightful measure or a dance;
        For gnarling sorrow hath less power to bite
        The man that mocks at it and sets it light.[22]

BULLING. O, who can hold a fire in his hand
        By thinking on the frosty Caucasus?
        Or cloy the hungry edge of appetite
        By bare imagination of a feast?
        Or wallow naked in December snow
        By thinking on fantastic summer's heat?
        O no, the apprehension of the good   300
        Gives but the greater feeling to the worse.
        Fell sorrow's tooth doth never rankle more
        Than when he bites but lanceth not the sore.

GAUNT   Come, come, my son, I'll bring thee on thy way;
        Had I thy youth and cause, I would not stay.

BULLING. Then England's ground farewell, sweet soil adieu,
        My mother and my nurse that bears me yet.
        Where'er I wander, boast of this I can:
        Though banished, yet a true-born Englishman.
                            [Exeunt.

SCENE 4.

London. The court.

Enter, at one door, the KING, BAGOT *and* GREENE,
and, at another door, LORD AUMERLE.

RICHARD   We did observe. – Cousin Aumerle,
How far brought you high Her'ford on his way?

AUMERLE   I brought high Her'ford, if you call him so,
But to the next high-way, and there I left him.

RICHARD   And say, what store of parting tears were shed?

AUMERLE   Faith, none for me; except the north-east wind,
Which then blew bitterly against our faces,
Awaked the sleeping rheum, and so by chance
Did grace our hollow parting with a tear.

RICHARD   What said our cousin when you parted with him?   10

AUMERLE   'Farewell';
And, for my heart disdainèd that my tongue
Should so profane the word, that taught me craft
To counterfeit oppression of such grief
That words seemed buried in my sorrow's grave.
Marry, would the word 'farewell' have
                              lengthened hours,
And added years to his short banishment,
He should have had a volume of farewells;
But since it would not, he had none of me.

RICHARD   He is our cousin, cousin,[23] but 'tis doubt,   20
When time shall call him home from banishment,
Whether our kinsman come to see his friends.
Ourself and Bushy, Bagot here and Greene[24]
Observed his courtship to the common people:
How he did seem to dive into their hearts
With humble and familiar courtesy;
What reverence he did throw away on slaves,
Wooing poor craftsmen with the craft of smiles
And patient underbearing of his fortune,
As 'twere to banish their affects with him.   30
Off goes his bonnet to an oyster-wench;
A brace of draymen bid God speed him well,

And had the tribute of his supple knee,
With 'Thanks, my countrymen, my loving friends';
As were our England in reversion his,
And he our subjects' next degree in hope.

GREENE   Well, he is gone; and with him go these thoughts.
– Now, for the rebels which stand out in Ireland,
Expedient manage must be made, my liege,
Ere further leisure yield them further means   40
For their advantage and your Highness' loss.

RICHARD   We will ourself in person to this war;
And, for our coffers with too great a court
And liberal largess are grown somewhat light,
We are enforced to farm our royal realm,
The revenue whereof shall furnish us
For our affairs in hand. If that come short,
Our substitutes at home shall have blank charters,
Whereto, when they shall know what men are rich,
They shall subscribe them for large sums of gold,   50
And send them after to supply our wants;
For we will make for Ireland presently.[25]

Enter BUSHY.

Bushy, what news?

BUSHY   Old John of Gaunt is grievous sick, my lord,
Suddenly taken, and hath sent post-haste
To entreat your Majesty to visit him.

RICHARD   Where lies he?

BUSHY   At Ely House.

RICHARD   Now put it, God, in the physician's mind
To help him to his grave immediately!   60
The lining of his coffers shall make coats
To deck our soldiers for these Irish wars.
Come, gentlemen, let's all go visit him:
Pray God we may make haste, and come too late!

ALL   Amen.   [*Exeunt.*

ACT 2, SCENE I.

London. Inside Ely House.

Enter JOHN OF GAUNT *(ill, and aided by* ATTENDANTS*)*
with the DUKE OF YORK.

GAUNT   Will the King come, that I may breathe my last
In wholesome counsel to his unstaid youth?

YORK   Vex not yourself, nor strive not with your breath,
For all in vain comes counsel to his ear.

GAUNT   O, but (they say) the tongues of dying men
Enforce attention, like deep harmony:
Where words are scarce, they are seldom spent in vain,
For they breathe truth that breathe their words in pain.
He that no more must say is listened more
   Than they whom youth and ease have taught to
                              glose;   10
More are men's ends marked than their lives before:
   The setting sun, and music at the close,
As the last taste of sweets, is sweetest last,
Writ in remembrance more than things long past.
Though Richard my life's counsel would not hear,
My death's sad tale may yet undeaf his ear.

YORK   No, it is stopped with other flattering sounds:
As praises, of whose taste th'unwise are fond; [26]
Lascivious metres, to whose venom sound
The open ear of youth doth always listen;   20
Report of fashions in proud Italy,
Whose manners still our tardy-apish nation
Limps after in base imitation.
Where doth the world thrust forth a vanity —
So it be new, there's no respect how vile —
That is not quickly buzzed into his ears?
Then all too late comes counsel to be heard,
Where will doth mutiny with wit's regard.
Direct not him whose way himself will choose;
'Tis breath thou lack'st, and that breath wilt thou lose.   30

GAUNT   Methinks I am a prophet new-inspired,

And thus, expiring, do foretell of him:
His rash fierce blaze of riot cannot last,
For violent fires soon burn out themselves;
Small showers last long, but sudden storms are short;
He tires betimes that spurs too fast betimes;
With eager feeding, food doth choke the feeder;
Light vanity, insatiate cormorant,
Consuming means, soon preys upon itself.
This royal throne of kings, this sceptred isle,   40
This earth of majesty, this seat of Mars,
This other Eden, demi-paradise,
This fortress built by nature for herself
Against infection and the hand of war,
This happy breed of men, this little world;
This precious stone set in the silver sea,
Which serves it in the office of a wall,
Or as a moat defensive to a house,
Against the envy of less happier lands;
This blessèd plot, this earth, this realm, this England,   50
This nurse, this teeming womb of royal kings,
Feared by their breed, and famous by their birth,
Renownèd for their deeds as far from home,
For Christian service and true chivalry,
As is the sepulchre in stubborn Jewry
Of the world's ransom, blessed Mary's son:[27]
This land of such dear souls, this dear dear land,
Dear for her reputation through the world,
Is now leased out (I die pronouncing it)
Like to a tenement or pelting farm.   60
England, bound in with the triumphant sea,
Whose rocky shore beats back the envious siege
Of wat'ry Neptune, is now bound in with shame,
With inky blots and rotten parchment bonds:
That England, that was wont to conquer others,
Hath made a shameful conquest of itself.
Ah, would the scandal vanish with my life,
How happy then were my ensuing death!

Enter KING, QUEEN, AUMERLE, BUSHY, GREENE,
BAGOT, ROSS *and* WILLOUGHBY.

YORK	The King is come; deal mildly with his youth,
	For young hot colts, being ragg'd, do rage the more.[28] 70
QUEEN	How fares our noble uncle, Lancaster?
RICHARD	What comfort, man? How is't with agèd Gaunt?
GAUNT	O, how that name befits my composition!
	Old Gaunt indeed, and gaunt in being old:
	Within me grief hath kept a tedious fast,
	And who abstains from meat that is not gaunt?
	For sleeping England long time have I watched;
	Watching breeds leanness, leanness is all gaunt.
	The pleasure that some fathers feed upon
	Is my strict fast: I mean, my children's looks; 80
	And, therein fasting, hast thou made me gaunt:
	Gaunt am I for the grave, gaunt as a grave,
	Whose hollow womb inherits nought but bones.
RICHARD	Can sick men play so nicely with their names?
GAUNT	No, misery makes sport to mock itself:
	Since thou dost seek to kill my name in me,[29]
	I mock my name, great King, to flatter thee.
RICHARD	Should dying men flatter with those that live?
GAUNT	No, no; men living flatter those that die.
RICHARD	Thou, now a-dying, say'st thou flatter'st me. 90
GAUNT	Oh no, thou diest, though I the sicker be.
RICHARD	I am in health, I breathe, and see thee ill.
GAUNT	Now He that made me knows I see thee ill,
	Ill in myself to see, and in thee seeing ill.[30]
	Thy death-bed is no lesser than thy land,
	Wherein thou liest in reputation sick,
	And thou, too careless patient as thou art,
	Commit'st thy anointed body to the cure
	Of those physicians that first wounded thee.[31]
	A thousand flatterers sit within thy crown, 100
	Whose compass is no bigger than thy head,
	And yet incagèd in so small a verge,
	The waste is no whit lesser than thy land.
	O, had thy grandsire with a prophet's eye
	Seen how his son's son should destroy his sons,
	From forth thy reach he would have laid thy shame,
	Deposing thee before thou wert possessed,

Which art possessed now to depose thyself.
Why, cousin, wert thou regent of the world,
It were a shame to let this land by lease;   110
But, for thy world, enjoying but this land,
Is it not more than shame to shame it so?
Landlord of England art thou now, not King,
Thy state of law is bondslave to the law,
And —

RICHARD   Thou, a lunatic lean-witted fool,
Presuming on an ague's privilege,
Dar'st with thy frozen admonition
Make pale our cheek, chasing the royal blood
With fury from his native residence.[32]
Now by my seat's right royal majesty,   120
Wert thou not brother to great Edward's son,
This tongue that runs so roundly in thy head
Should run thy head from thy unreverent shoulders.

GAUNT   O spare me not, my brother Edward's son,
For that I was his father Edward's son;
That blood already, like the pelican,
Hast thou tapped out and drunkenly caroused.[33]
My brother Gloucester, plain well-meaning soul
(Whom fair befall in heaven 'mongst happy souls),
May be a precedent and witness good   130
That thou respect'st not spilling Edward's blood.
Join with the present sickness that I have,
And thy unkindness be like crookèd age,
To crop at once a too-long-withered flower.
Live in thy shame, but die not shame with thee;
These words hereafter thy tormentors be!
Convey me to my bed, then to my grave:
Love they to live, that love and honour have.
                    [*Exit Gaunt, aided by attendants.*

RICHARD And let them die, that age and sullens have;
For both hast thou, and both become the grave.   140

YORK   I do beseech your Majesty, impute his words
To wayward sickliness and age in him.
He loves you, on my life, and holds you dear
As Harry Duke of Her'ford, were he here.

RICHARD   Right, you say true: as Her'ford's love, so his;
          As theirs, so mine; and all be as it is.[34]

                Enter NORTHUMBERLAND.

NORTH.   My liege, old Gaunt commends him to your Majesty.
RICHARD   What says he?
NORTH.   Nay, nothing; all is said:
          His tongue is now a stringless instrument;
          Words, life, and all, old Lancaster hath spent.   150
YORK   Be York the next that must be bankrupt so!
          Though death be poor, it ends a mortal woe.
RICHARD   The ripest fruit first falls, and so doth he;
          His time is spent, our pilgrimage must be;
          So much for that. Now for our Irish wars:
          We must supplant those rough rug-headed kerns,
          Which live like venom, where no venom else
          But only they have privilege to live.[35]
          And, for these great affairs do ask some charge,
          Towards our assistance we do seize to us   160
          The plate, coin, revenues, and moveables,
          Whereof our uncle Gaunt did stand possessed.
YORK   How long shall I be patient? Ah, how long
          Shall tender duty make me suffer wrong?
          Not Gloucester's death, nor Her'ford's banishment,
          Not Gaunt's rebukes, nor England's private wrongs,
          Nor the prevention of poor Bullingbrooke
          About his marriage, nor my own disgrace,
          Have ever made me sour my patient cheek,
          Or bend one wrinkle on my sovereign's face.[36]   170
          I am the last of noble Edward's sons,
          Of whom thy father, Prince of Wales, was first.
          In war was never lion raged more fierce,
          In peace was never gentle lamb more mild,
          Than was that young and princely gentleman.
          His face thou hast, for even so looked he,
          Accomplished with the number of thy hours;
          But when he frowned, it was against the French,
          And not against his friends; his noble hand
          Did win what he did spend, and spent not that   180

Which his triumphant father's hand had won;
His hands were guilty of no kindred blood,
But bloody with the enemies of his kin.
O Richard, York is too far gone with grief,
Or else he never would compare between –

RICHARD   Why, uncle, what's the matter?

YORK   O my liege,
Pardon me, if you please; if not, I, pleased
Not to be pardoned, am content withal.
Seek you to seize and gripe into your hands
The royalties and rights of banished Her'ford?   190
Is not Gaunt dead? And doth not Her'ford live?
Was not Gaunt just? And is not Harry true?
Did not the one deserve to have an heir?
Is not his heir a well-deserving son?
Take Her'ford's rights away, and take from Time
His charters and his customary rights;
Let not tomorrow then ensue today;
Be not thyself: for how art thou a king
But by fair sequence and succession?
Now, afore God – God forbid I say true! –   200
If you do wrongfully seize Her'ford's rights,
Call in the letters-patents that he hath
By his attorneys-general to sue
His livery, and deny his offered homage,[37]
You pluck a thousand dangers on your head,
You lose a thousand well-disposèd hearts,
And prick my tender patience to those thoughts
Which honour and allegiance cannot think.

RICHARD   Think what you will, we seize into our hands
His plate, his goods, his money and his lands.   210

YORK   I'll not be by the while. My liege, farewell.
What will ensue hereof there's none can tell;
But by bad courses may be understood,
That their events can never fall out good.   [Exit.

RICHARD   Go, Bushy, to the Earl of Wiltshire straight:
Bid him repair to us to Ely House,
To see this business. Tomorrow next
We will for Ireland, and 'tis time, I trow.

And we create, in absence of ourself,
Our uncle York Lord Governor of England;   220
For he is just, and always loved us well.
– Come on, our Queen; tomorrow must we part;
Be merry, for our time of stay is short.

> [*Exeunt the King and Queen, followed by*
> *Bushy, Aumerle, Greene, and Bagot.*

NORTH.   Well, lords, the Duke of Lancaster is dead.

ROSS   And living too, for now his son is Duke.

WILL.   Barely in title, not in revenues.

NORTH.   Richly in both, if justice had her right.

ROSS   My heart is great, but it must break with silence,
          Ere't be disburdened with a liberal tongue.

NORTH.   Nay, speak thy mind, and let him ne'er speak more   230
          That speaks thy words again to do thee harm.

WILL.   Tends that thou wouldst speak to the Duke of
                                                Her'ford?
          If it be so, out with it boldly, man.
          Quick is mine ear to hear of good towards him.

ROSS   No good at all that I can do for him,
          Unless you call it good to pity him,
          Bereft, and gelded of his patrimony.

NORTH.   Now afore God, 'tis shame such wrongs are borne
          In him, a royal prince, and many moe
          Of noble blood in this declining land.   240
          The King is not himself, but basely led
          By flatterers; and what they will inform,
          Merely in hate, 'gainst any of us all,
          That will the King severely prosecute
          'Gainst us, our lives, our children, and our heirs.

ROSS   The commons hath he pilled with grievous taxes,
          And quite lost their hearts. The nobles hath he fined
          For ancient quarrels, and quite lost their hearts.

WILL.   And daily new exactions are devised,
          As blanks, benevolences, and I wot not what;   250
          But what, a God's name, doth become of this?

NORTH.   Wars hath not wasted it, for warred he hath not,
          But basely yielded upon compromise
          That which his noble ancestors achieved with blows.[38]

More hath he spent in peace than they in wars.

ROSS   The Earl of Wiltshire hath the realm in farm.

WILL.   The King's grown bankrupt like a broken man.

NORTH. Reproach and dissolution hangeth over him.

ROSS   He hath not money for these Irish wars,
His burthenous taxations notwithstanding,   260
But by the robbing of the banished Duke.

NORTH. His noble kinsman. Most degenerate King!
But, lords, we hear this fearful tempest sing,
Yet seek no shelter to avoid the storm;
We see the wind sit sore upon our sails,
And yet we strike not, but securely perish.

ROSS   We see the very wrack that we must suffer,
And unavoided is the danger now
For suffering so the causes of our wrack.

NORTH. Not so: even through the hollow eyes of death   270
I spy life peering, but I dare not say
How near the tidings of our comfort is.

WILL.   Nay, let us share thy thoughts, as thou dost ours.

ROSS   Be confident to speak, Northumberland.
We three are but thyself, and, speaking so,
Thy words are but as thoughts: therefore be bold.

NORTH. Then thus: I have from le Port Blanc, a bay
In Brittany, received intelligence
That Harry Duke of Her'ford, Rainold Lord Cobham,
Thomas, the Earl of Arundel's son and heir,[39]   280
That late broke from the Duke of Exeter,
His brother, Archbishop late of Canterbury,
Sir Thomas Erpingham, Sir John Ramston,
Sir John Norbery, Sir Robert Waterton, and
                                    Francis Coint –
All these, well furnished by the Duke of Brittaine,
With eight tall ships, three thousand men of war,
Are making hither with all due expedience,
And shortly mean to touch our northern shore.
Perhaps they had ere this, but that they stay
The first departing of the King for Ireland.   290
If then we shall shake off our slavish yoke,
Imp out our drooping country's broken wing,

Redeem from broking pawn the blemished crown,
Wipe off the dust that hides our sceptre's gilt,
And make high majesty look like itself,
Away with me in post to Ravenspurgh;
But if you faint, as fearing to do so,
Stay and be secret, and myself will go.

ROSS   To horse, to horse! Urge doubts to them that fear.

WILL.   Hold out my horse, and I will first be there.   [*Exeunt.* 300

SCENE 2.

Inside Windsor Castle.

Enter the QUEEN, BUSHY *and* BAGOT.

BUSHY   Madam, your Majesty is too much sad.
You promised, when you parted with the King,
To lay aside life-harming heaviness
And entertain a cheerful disposition.

QUEEN   To please the King I did; to please myself
I cannot do it; yet I know no cause
Why I should welcome such a guest as grief,
Save bidding farewell to so sweet a guest
As my sweet Richard. Yet again methinks
Some unborn sorrow, ripe in Fortune's womb,   10
Is coming towards me; and my inward soul
With nothing trembles, at some thing it grieves,
More than with parting from my lord the King.

BUSHY   Each substance of a grief hath twenty shadows,
Which shows like grief itself, but is not so;
For Sorrow's eye, glazèd with blinding tears,
Divides one thing entire to many objects:
Like pérspectives,[40] which, rightly gazed upon,
Show nothing but confusion; eyed awry,
Distinguish form. So your sweet Majesty,   20
Looking awry upon your lord's departure,
Find shapes of grief more than himself to wail,
Which, looked on as it is, is nought but shadows
Of what it is not. Then, thrice-gracious Queen,

          More than your lord's departure weep not. More's
                                not seen,[41]
          Or if it be, 'tis with false Sorrow's eye,
          Which, for things true, weeps things imaginary.

QUEEN   It may be so; but yet my inward soul
          Persuades me it is otherwise. Howe'er it be,
          I cannot but be sad; so heavy sad,   30
          As (though, on thinking, on no thought I think)
          Makes me with heavy nothing faint and shrink.

BUSHY   'Tis nothing but conceit, my gracious lady.

QUEEN   'Tis nothing less: conceit is still derived
          From some forefather grief; mine is not so,
          For nothing hath begot my something grief,
          Or something hath the nothing that I grieve;
          'Tis in reversion that I do possess;
          But what it is that is not yet known, what
          I cannot name, 'tis nameless woe, I wot.[42]   40

                    Enter GREENE.

GREENE   God save your Majesty, and well met, gentlemen.
          I hope the King is not yet shipped for Ireland.

QUEEN   Why hopest thou so? 'Tis better hope he is,
          For his designs crave haste, his haste good hope;
          Then wherefore dost thou hope he is not shipped?

GREENE   That he, our hope, might have retired his power,
          And driven into despair an enemy's hope,
          Who strongly hath set footing in this land.
          The banished Bullingbrooke repeals himself,
          And with uplifted arms is safe arrived   50
          At Ravenspurgh.

QUEEN   Now God in heaven forbid!

GREENE   Ah madam, 'tis too true; and, that is worse,
          The Lord Northumberland, his son young
                                 Henry Percy,
          The Lords of Ross, Beaumond, and Willoughby,
          With all their powerful friends, are fled to him.

BUSHY   Why have you not proclaimed Northumberland
          And the rest of the revolted faction traitors?

GREENE   We have, whereupon the Earl of Worcester

	Hath broke his staff, resigned his stewardship,
	And all the household servants fled with him 60
	To Bullingbrooke.
QUEEN	So, Greene, thou art the midwife to my woe,
	And Bullingbrooke my sorrow's dismal heir.
	Now hath my soul brought forth her prodigy,
	And I, a gasping new-delivered mother,
	Have woe to woe, sorrow to sorrow joined.
BUSHY	Despair not, madam.
QUEEN	Who shall hinder me?
	I will despair, and be at enmity
	With cozening Hope: he is a flatterer,
	A parasite, a keeper-back of Death, 70
	Who gently would dissolve the bands of life,
	Which false Hope lingers in extremity.

Enters YORK, *wearing a gorget.*

GREENE	Here comes the Duke of York.
QUEEN	With signs of war about his agèd neck.
	O, full of careful business are his looks!
	– Uncle, for God's sake, speak comfortable words.
YORK	Should I do so, I should belie my thoughts.
	Comfort's in heaven, and we are on the earth,
	Where nothing lives but crosses, cares and grief.
	Your husband, he is gone to save far off, 80
	Whilst others come to make him lose at home.
	Here am I left to underprop his land,
	Who, weak with age, cannot support myself.
	Now comes the sick hour that his surfeit made;
	Now shall he try his friends that flattered him.

Enter a male SERVANT.

SERVANT	My lord, your son was gone before I came.
YORK	He was? Why, so: go all which way it will!
	The nobles they are fled, the commons they are cold,[43]
	And will (I fear) revolt on Her'ford's side.
	Sirra, get thee to Plashie, to my sister Gloucester, 90
	Bid her send me presently a thousand pound.
	Hold, take my ring.
SERVANT	My lord, I had forgot to tell your lordship:

Today, as I came by, I callèd there –
But I shall grieve you to report the rest.

YORK   What is't, knave?

SERVANT   An hour before I came, the Duchess died.

YORK   God for his mercy, what a tide of woes
Comes rushing on this woeful land at once!
I know not what to do; I would to God   100
(So my untruth had not provoked him to it),
The King had cut off my head with my brother's.
What, are there no posts dispatched for Ireland?
How shall we do for money for these wars?
– Come, sister – cousin, I would say; pray pardon me.[44]
– Go, fellow, get thee home, provide some carts,
And bring away the armour that is there.
                                        [Exit servant.
– Gentlemen, will you go muster men? If I
Know how or which way to order these affairs,
Thus thrust disorderly into my hands,   110
Never believe me. Both are my kinsmen:
Th'one is my Sovereign, whom both my oath
And duty bids defend; th'other again
Is my kinsman, whom the King hath wronged,
Whom conscience and my kindred bids to right.
Well, somewhat we must do. – Come, cousin, I'll
Dispose of you. – Gentlemen, go muster up your men,
And meet me presently at Berkeley Castle.
I should to Plashie too, but time will not permit:
All is uneven, and everything is left   120
At six and seven.[45]   [Exeunt York and the Queen.

BUSHY   The wind sits fair for news to go to Ireland,
But none returns. For us to levy power
Proportionable to the enemy
Is all unpossible.

GREENE   Besides, our nearness to the King in love
Is near the hate of those love not the King.

BAGOT   And that is the wavering commons, for their love
Lies in their purses; and whoso empties them,
By so much fills their hearts with deadly hate.   130

BUSHY   Wherein the King stands generally condemned.

BAGOT   If judgement lie in them, then so do we,
          Because we ever have been near the King.
GREENE   Well, I will for refuge straight to Bristol Castle;
          The Earl of Wiltshire is already there.
BUSHY   Thither will I with you, for little office
          The hateful commons will perform for us,
          Except like curs to tear us all to pieces.
          [To Bagot:] Will you go along with us?
BAGOT   No, I will to Ireland, to his Majesty.   140
          Farewell. If heart's presages be not vain,
          We three here part that ne'er shall meet again.
BUSHY   That's as York thrives to beat back Bullingbrooke.
GREENE   Alas, poor Duke: the task he undertakes
          Is numb'ring sands and drinking oceans dry.
          Where one on his side fights, thousands will fly.
          Farewell at once, for once, for all, and ever.
BUSHY   Well, we may meet again.
BAGOT   I fear me, never.
          [Exeunt Bushy and Greene in one direction;
                              exit Bagot in another.

                          SCENE 3.

          Gloucestershire. Near Berkeley Castle.

          Enter BULLINGBROOKE and NORTHUMBERLAND.

BULLING. How far is it, my lord, to Berkeley now?
NORTH.   Believe me, noble lord,
          I am a stranger here in Gloucestershire.
          These high wild hills and rough uneven ways
          Draws out our miles and makes them wearisome;
          And yet your fair discourse hath been as sugar,
          Making the hard way sweet and délectable.
          But I bethink me what a weary way
          From Ravenspurgh to Cotshall will be found
          In Ross and Willoughby, wanting your company,   10
          Which I protest hath very much beguiled
          The tediousness and process of my travel;
          But theirs is sweetened with the hope to have

The present benefit which I possess,
And hope to joy is little less in joy
Than hope enjoyed. By this the weary lords
Shall make their way seem short, as mine hath done
By sight of what I have, your noble company.

BULLING. Of much less value is my company
Than your good words. – But who comes here?   20

Enter HARRY PERCY.

NORTH. It is my son, young Harry Percy,
Sent from my brother Worcester, whencesoever.
– Harry, how fares your uncle?

PERCY I had thought, my lord, to have learned his
                                        health of you.

NORTH. Why, is he not with the Queen?

PERCY No, my good lord, he hath forsook the court,
Broken his staff of office, and dispersed
The household of the King.

NORTH.   What was his reason?
He was not so resolved, when last we spake together.

PERCY Because your lordship was proclaimèd traitor.   30
But he, my lord, is gone to Ravenspurgh,
To offer service to the Duke of Her'ford,
And sent me over by Berkeley to discover
What power the Duke of York had levied there,
Then with directions to repair to Ravenspurgh.

NORTH. Have you forgot the Duke of Her'ford, boy?

PERCY No, my good lord, for that is not forgot
Which ne'er I did remember: to my knowledge,
I never in my life did look on him.

NORTH. Then learn to know him now. This is the Duke.   40

PERCY My gracious lord, I tender you my service,
Such as it is, being tender, raw, and young;
Which elder days shall ripen and confirm
To more approvèd service and desert.

BULLING. I thank thee, gentle Percy, and be sure
I count myself in nothing else so happy
As in a soul rememb'ring my good friends;
And as my fortune ripens with thy love,
It shall be still thy true love's recompense.

My heart this covenant makes, my hand thus seals it.   50
                        [*He clasps Percy's hand.*

NORTH.   How far is it to Berkeley? And what stir
           Keeps good old York there with his men of war?
PERCY   There stands the castle, by yon tuft of trees,
           Manned with three hundred men, as I have heard,
           And in it are the Lords of York, Berkeley, and Seymour;
           None else of name and noble estimate.

                Enter ROSS *and* WILLOUGHBY.

NORTH.   Here come the Lords of Ross and Willoughby,
           Bloody with spurring, fiery-red with haste.
BULLING.   Welcome, my lords. I wot your love pursues
           A banished traitor: all my treasury   60
           Is yet but unfelt thanks, which, more enriched,
           Shall be your love and labour's recompense.
ROSS   Your presence makes us rich, most noble lord.
WILL.   And far surmounts our labour to attain it.
BULLING.   Evermore thanks, the exchequer of the poor,
           Which, till my infant fortune comes to years,
           Stands for my bounty. – But who comes here?

                    Enter BERKELEY.

NORTH.   It is my Lord of Berkeley, as I guess.
BERKELEY   My Lord of Her'ford, my message is to you.
BULLING.   My lord, my answer is to 'Lancaster',[46]   70
           And I am come to seek that name in England;
           And I must find that title in your tongue,
           Before I make reply to aught you say.
BERKELEY   Mistake me not, my lord, 'tis not my meaning
           To raze one title of your honour out.
           To you, my lord, I come, what lord you will,
           From the most gracious regent of this land,
           The Duke of York, to know what pricks you on
           To take advantage of the absent time
           And fright our native peace with self-borne arms.   80

                      Enter YORK.

BULLING.   I shall not need transport my words by you;
           Here comes his Grace in person.
           [*He kneels to York.*]   My noble uncle!

YORK   Show me thy humble heart, and not thy knee,
            Whose duty is deceivable and false.
BULLING.   My gracious uncle –
YORK   Tut, tut! Grace me no grace, nor uncle me no uncle,
            I am no traitor's uncle, and that word 'grace'
            In an ungracious mouth is but profane.
            Why have those banished and forbidden legs
            Dared once to touch a dust of England's ground?   90
            But then more 'why?': why have they dared to march
            So many miles upon her peaceful bosom,
            Frighting her pale-faced villages with war,
            And ostentation of despisèd arms?
            Com'st thou because th'anointed King is hence?
            Why, foolish boy, the King is left behind,
            And in my loyal bosom lies his power.
            Were I but now the lord of such hot youth
            As when brave Gaunt, thy father, and myself,
            Rescued the Black Prince, that young Mars of men,   100
            From forth the ranks of many thousand French,
            O then how quickly should this arm of mine,
            Now prisoner to the palsy, chástise thee,
            And minister correction to thy fault!
BULLING.   My gracious uncle, let me know my fault:
            On what condition stands it and wherein?
YORK   Even in condition of the worst degree:
            In gross rebellion and detested treason.
            Thou art a banished man, and here art come,
            Before the expiration of thy time,   110
            In braving arms against thy Sovereign.
BULLING.   [rising:] As I was banished, I was banished Her'ford,
            But as I come, I come for Lancaster.
            And, noble uncle, I beseech your Grace,
            Look on my wrongs with an indifferent eye.
            You are my father, for methinks in you
            I see old Gaunt alive. O then my father,
            Will you permit that I shall stand condemned
            A wand'ring vagabond, my rights and royalties
            Plucked from my arms perforce, and given away   120
            To upstart unthrifts? Wherefore was I born?

If that my cousin King be King in England,
It must be granted I am Duke of Lancaster.
You have a son, Aumerle, my noble cousin;
Had you first died, and he been thus trod down,
He should have found his uncle Gaunt a father
To rouse his wrongs and chase them to the bay.
I am denied to sue my livery here,
And yet my letters-patents give me leave.
My father's goods are all distrained and sold,   130
And these and all are all-amiss employed.
What would you have me do? I am a subject;
And I challenge law. Attorneys are denied me,
And therefore personally I lay my claim
To my inheritance of free descent.

NORTH. The noble Duke hath been too much abused.
ROSS   It stands your Grace upon to do him right;
WILL.   Base men by his endowments are made great.
YORK   My lords of England, let me tell you this:
        I have had feeling of my cousin's wrongs,   140
        And laboured all I could to do him right;
        But in this kind to come, in braving arms,
        Be his own carver and cut out his way,
        To find out right with wrong: it may not be;
        And you that do abet him in this kind
        Cherish rebellion, and are rebels all.

NORTH. The noble Duke hath sworn his coming is
        But for his own; and, for the right of that,
        We all have strongly sworn to give him aid;
        And let him never see joy that breaks that oath!   150
YORK   Well, well, I see the issue of these arms.
        I cannot mend it, I must needs confess,
        Because my power is weak and all ill-left;
        But if I could, by Him that gave me life,
        I would attach you all, and make you stoop
        Unto the sovereign mercy of the King;
        But, since I cannot, be it known unto you,
        I do remain as neuter. So, fare you well;
        Unless you please to enter in the castle,
        And there repose you for this night.   160

BULLING. An offer, uncle, that we will accept.
           But we must win your Grace to go with us
           To Bristow Castle, which they say is held
           By Bushy, Bagot and their complices,
           The caterpillars of the commonwealth,
           Which I have sworn to weed and pluck away.
YORK   It may be I will go with you; but yet I'll pause,
           For I am loath to break our country's laws.
           Nor friends nor foes, to me welcome you are:
           Things past redress are now with me past care. [*Exeunt.* 170

SCENE 4.

A camp in Wales.

Enter the EARL OF SALISBURY *and a Welsh* CAPTAIN.

CAPTAIN   My Lord of Salisbury, we have stayed ten days,
           And hardly kept our countrymen together,
           And yet we hear no tidings from the King;
           Therefore we will disperse ourselves. Farewell.
SALISBURY Stay yet another day, thou trusty Welshman;
           The King reposeth all his confidence in thee.
CAPTAIN   'Tis thought the King is dead; we will not stay.
           The bay-trees in our country are all withered,
           And meteors fright the fixèd stars of heaven;[47]
           The pale-faced moon looks bloody on the earth,   10
           And lean-looked prophets whisper fearful change;
           Rich men look sad, and ruffians dance and leap:
           The one in fear to lose what they enjoy,
           The other to enjoy by rage and war.
           These signs fore-run the death or fall of kings.
           Farewell. Our countrymen are gone and fled,
           As well assured Richard their King is dead.   [*Exit.*
SALISBURY Ah Richard! With the eyes of heavy mind,
           I see thy glory, like a shooting star,
           Fall to the base earth from the firmament.   20
           Thy sun sets weeping in the lowly west,
           Witnessing storms to come, woe, and unrest.
           Thy friends are fled to wait upon thy foes,
           And crossly to thy good all fortune goes.   [*Exit.*

ACT 3, SCENE 1.

Bristol. Outside the castle.

Enter BULLINGBROOKE, YORK, NORTHUMBERLAND, ROSS, PERCY *and*
WILLOUGHBY, *with* SOLDIERS *guarding* BUSHY *and* GREENE.

BULLING. Bring forth these men. [*Bushy and Greene are led to him.*
     – Bushy and Greene, I will not vex your souls
     (Since presently your souls must part your bodies)
     With too much urging your pernicious lives,
     For 'twere no charity; yet, to wash your blood
     From off my hands, here in the view of men
     I will unfold some causes of your deaths.
     You have misled a prince, a royal king,
     A happy gentleman in blood and lineaments,
     By you unhappied and disfigured clean.   10
     You have, in manner, with your sinful hours
     Made a divorce betwixt his Queen and him,
     Broke the possession of a royal bed,[48]
     And stained the beauty of a fair queen's cheeks
     With tears drawn from her eyes by your foul wrongs.
     Myself (a prince by fortune of my birth,
     Near to the King in blood, and near in love
     Till you did make him misinterpret me)
     Have stooped my neck under your injuries,
     And sighed my English breath in foreign clouds,   20
     Eating the bitter bread of banishment,
     Whilst you have fed upon my signories,
     Disparked my parks, and felled my forest woods;
     From my own windows torn my household coat,
     Razed out my impresse, leaving me no sign
     (Save men's opinions and my living blood)
     To show the world I am a gentleman.
     This and much more, much more than twice all this,
     Condemns you to the death. [*To soldiers:*] See them
                                delivered over
     To execution and the hand of death.   30

BUSHY   More welcome is the stroke of death to me

Than Bullingbrooke to England. Lords, farewell.

GREENE   My comfort is, that heaven will take our souls,
And plague injustice with the pains of hell.

BULLING.   My Lord Northumberland, see them dispatched.

> [Exeunt Northumberland and soldiers
> with Bushy and Greene.

– Uncle, you say the Queen is at your house:
For God's sake, fairly let her be entreated.
Tell her I send to her my kind commends;
Take special care my greetings be delivered.

YORK   A gentleman of mine I have dispatched   40
With letters of your love to her at large.

BULLING.   Thanks, gentle uncle. – Come, lords, away,
To fight with Glendo'r and his complices.
Awhile to work, and, after, holiday.   [Exeunt.

SCENE 2.

The coast of Wales, near Harlech Castle.

Drumming and a flourish heard. Enter KING RICHARD, *the* BISHOP
OF CARLISLE, AUMERLE, *and* SOLDIERS *(some bearing colours).*

RICHARD   Barkloughly Castle call they this at hand?49

AUMERLE   Yea, my lord. How brooks your Grace the air,
After your late tossing on the breaking seas?

RICHARD   Needs must I like it well. I weep for joy
To stand upon my kingdom once again.
[He stoops.] Dear earth, I do salute thee with my hand,
Though rebels wound thee with their horses' hoofs.
As a long-parted mother with her child
Plays fondly with her tears and smiles in meeting,
So, weeping, smiling, greet I thee, my earth,   10
And do thee favours with my royal hands.
Feed not thy sovereign's foe, my gentle earth,
Nor with thy sweets comfort his ravenous sense,
But let thy spiders that suck up thy venom,
And heavy-gaited toads, lie in their way,
Doing annoyance to the treacherous feet
Which with usurping steps do trample thee.

Yield stinging nettles to mine enemies;
And when they from thy bosom pluck a flower,
Guard it, I pray thee, with a lurking adder,   20
Whose double tongue may with a mortal touch
Throw death upon thy Sovereign's enemies.
[*He rises.*] Mock not my senseless conjuration, lords;
This earth shall have a feeling, and these stones
Prove armèd soldiers, ere her native King
Shall falter under foul rebellion's arms.

CARLISLE Fear not, my lord. That Power that made you King
Hath power to keep you King in spite of all.
The means that heaven yields must be embraced,
And not neglected; else, if heaven would   30
And we will not, heaven's offer we refuse,
The proffered means of succour and redress.[50]

AUMERLE He means, my lord, that we are too remiss,
Whilst Bullingbrooke, through our security,
Grows strong and great in substance and in power.

RICHARD Discomfortable cousin, know'st thou not
That when the searching eye of heaven is hid
(Behind the globe), that lights the lower world,
Then thieves and robbers range abroad unseen,
In murthers and in outrage, boldly, here;[51]   40
But when from under this terrestrial ball
He fires the proud tops of the eastern pines,
And darts his light through every guilty hole,
Then murders, treasons and detested sins
(The cloak of night being plucked from off their backs)
Stand bare and naked, trembling at themselves?
So when this thief, this traitor Bullingbrooke,
Who all this while hath revelled in the night
Whilst we were wand'ring with the Antipodes,[52]
Shall see us rising in our throne, the east,   50
His treasons will sit blushing in his face,
Not able to endure the sight of day,
But, self-affrighted, tremble at his sin.
Not all the water in the rough rude sea
Can wash the balm from an anointed king.[53]
The breath of worldly men cannot depose

The deputy elected by the Lord.
For every man that Bullingbrooke hath pressed
To lift shrewd steel against our golden crown,
God for his Richard hath in heavenly pay   60
A glorious angel; then, if angels fight,
Weak men must fall, for heaven still guards the right.

Enter SALISBURY.

Welcome, my lord: how far off lies your power?
SALISBURY Nor nea'r nor farther off, my gracious lord,
Than this weak arm. Discomfort guides my tongue,
And bids me speak of nothing but despair.
One day too late, I fear me, noble lord,
Hath clouded all thy happy days on earth.
O call back yesterday, bid time return,
And thou shalt have twelve thousand fighting men;   70
Today, today, unhappy day too late,
O'erthrows thy joys, friends, fortune and thy state;
For all the Welshmen, hearing thou wert dead,
Are gone to Bullingbrooke, dispersed, and fled.
AUMERLE   Comfort, my liege; why looks your Grace so pale?
RICHARD   But now the blood of twenty thousand men
Did triumph in my face, and they are fled;
And till so much blood thither come again,
Have I not reason to look pale and dead?
All souls that will be safe, fly from my side,   80
For time hath set a blot upon my pride.
AUMERLE   Comfort, my liege, remember who you are.
RICHARD   I had forgot myself. Am I not King?
Awake, thou coward majesty! Thou sleep'st.
Is not the King's name twenty thousand names?[54]
Arm, arm, my name! A puny subject strikes
At thy great glory. Look not to the ground,
Ye favourites of a king: are we not high?
High be our thoughts. I know my uncle York
Hath power enough to serve our turn. – But who
                               comes here?   90

Enter SCROOPE.

SCROOPE   More health and happiness betide my liege

Than can my care-tuned tongue deliver him.

RICHARD   Mine ear is open, and my heart prepared;
The worst is worldly loss thou canst unfold.
Say, is my kingdom lost? Why, 'twas my care,
And what loss is it to be rid of care?
Strives Bullingbrooke to be as great as we?
Greater he shall not be. If he serve God,
We'll serve Him too, and be his fellow so.
Revolt our subjects? That we cannot mend: 100
They break their faith to God as well as us.
Cry woe, destruction, ruin, and decay?[55]
The worst is death, and death will have his day.

SCROOPE   Glad am I that your Highness is so armed
To bear the tidings of calamity.
Like an unseasonable stormy day,
Which makes the silver rivers drown their shores
As if the world were all dissolved to tears,
So high above his limits swells the rage
Of Bullingbrooke, covering your fearful land   110
With hard bright steel, and hearts harder than steel.
White-beards have armed their thin and hairless scalps
Against thy majesty; boys, with women's voices,
Strive to speak big and clap their female joints
In stiff unwieldy arms against thy crown;
Thy very beadsmen learn to bend their bows
Of double-fatal yew against thy state;
Yea, distaff-women manage rusty bills
Against thy seat:[56] both young and old rebel,
And all goes worse than I have power to tell.   120

RICHARD   Too well, too well thou tell'st a tale so ill.
Where is the Earl of Wiltshire, where is Bagot,
What is become of Bushy, where is Greene,
That they have let the dangerous enemy
Measure our confines with such peaceful steps?
If we prevail, their heads shall pay for it.
I warrant they have made peace with Bullingbrooke.

SCROOPE   Peace have they made with him indeed, my lord.

RICHARD   O villains, vipers, damned without redemption!
Dogs, easily won to fawn on any man!   130

Snakes, in my heart-blood warmed, that sting my heart!
Three Judases, each one thrice worse than Judas!
Would they make peace? Terrible hell make war
Upon their spotted souls for this offence![57]

SCROOPE Sweet love, I see, changing his property,
Turns to the sourest and most deadly hate.
Again uncurse their souls: their peace is made
With heads and not with hands; those whom you curse
Have felt the worst of death's destroying wound,
And lie full low, graved in the hollow ground.   140

AUMERLE Is Bushy, Greene, and the Earl of Wiltshire dead?

SCROOPE Ay, all of them at Bristow lost their heads.

AUMERLE Where is the Duke my father with his power?

RICHARD No matter where; of comfort no man speak.
Let's talk of graves, of worms and epitaphs,
Make dust our paper, and with rainy eyes
Write sorrow on the bosom of the earth.
Let's choose executors and talk of wills;
And yet not so, for what can we bequeath,
Save our deposèd bodies to the ground?   150
Our lands, our lives and all are Bullingbrooke's,
And nothing can we call our own, but death,
And that small model of the barren earth
Which serves as paste and cover to our bones.[58]
[He sits.] For God's sake let us sit upon the ground,
And tell sad stories of the death of kings:
How some have been deposed, some slain in war,
Some haunted by the ghosts they have deposed,
Some poisoned by their wives, some sleeping killed;
All murthered: for, within the hollow crown   160
That rounds the mortal temples of a king,
Keeps Death his court, and there the antic sits,
Scoffing his state and grinning at his pomp,
Allowing him a breath, a little scene,
To monarchise, be feared, and kill with looks,
Infusing him with self and vain conceit,
As if this flesh which walls about our life
Were brass impregnable; and, humoured thus,
Comes at the last, and with a little pin

Bores through his castle wall, and – farewell, King!   170
Cover your heads, and mock not flesh and blood
With solemn reverence; throw away respect,
Tradition, form, and ceremonious duty;
For you have but mistook me all this while:
I live with bread like you, feel want,
Taste grief, need friends: subjected thus,
How can you say to me, I am a king?

CARLISLE   My lord, wise men ne'er sit and wail their woes,
But presently prevent the ways to wail.
To fear the foe, since fear oppresseth strength,   180
Gives, in your weakness, strength unto your foe,
And so your follies fight against yourself.
Fear and be slain: no worse can come. To fight
And fight and die is death destroying Death,
Where fearing dying pays Death servile breath.[59]

AUMERLE   My father hath a power: inquire of him,
And learn to make a body of a limb.

RICHARD   [rising:] Thou chid'st me well. Proud Bullingbrooke,
                                                            I come
To change blows with thee for our day of doom.
This ague-fit of fear is over-blown;   190
An easy task it is to win our own.
Say, Scroope, where lies our uncle with his power?
Speak sweetly, man, although thy looks be sour.

SCROOPE   Men judge by the complexion of the sky
                The state and inclination of the day;
So may you, by my dull and heavy eye,
                My tongue hath but a heavier tale to say.
I play the torturer, by small and small
To lengthen out the worst that must be spoken:
Your uncle York is joined with Bullingbrooke,   200
And all your northern castles yielded up,
And all your southern gentlemen in arms
Upon his party.[60]

RICHARD   Thou hast said enough.
[To Aumerle:] Beshrew thee, cousin, which didst lead
                                                            me forth
Of that sweet way I was in to despair.

What say you now? What comfort have we now?
By heaven, I'll hate him everlastingly
That bids me be of comfort any more.
Go to Flint Castle; there I'll pine away:
A king, woe's slave, shall kingly woe obey.   210
That power I have, discharge, and let them go
To ear the land that hath some hope to grow,
For I have none. Let no man speak again
To alter this, for counsel is but vain.

AUMERLE My liege, one word.

RICHARD   He does me double wrong
That wounds me with the flatteries of his tongue.
– Discharge my followers; let them hence away,
From Richard's night to Bullingbrooke's fair day.

                                                    [*Exeunt.*

SCENE 3.

Wales. Outside Flint Castle.

Enter, *marching*, BULLINGBROOKE, YORK, NORTHUMBERLAND,
and SOLDIERS *(some bearing colours) including a* DRUMMER *and*
a TRUMPETER. *Drumming ceases as they halt.*

BULLING. So that by this intelligence we learn
The Welshmen are dispersed, and Salisbury
Is gone to meet the King, who lately landed
With some few private friends upon this coast.

NORTH. The news is very fair and good, my lord.
Richard not far from hence hath hid his head.

YORK It would beseem the Lord Northumberland
To say '*King* Richard'. Alack the heavy day,
When such a sacred king should hide his head.

NORTH. Your Grace mistakes: only to be brief   10
Left I his title out.

YORK   The time hath been,
Would you have been so brief with him, he would
Have been so brief with you, to shorten you,
For taking so the head, your whole head's length.

BULLING. Mistake not, uncle, further than you should.

YORK   Take not, good cousin, further than you should,
            Lest *you* mistake: the heavens are o'er our heads.
BULLING.   I know it, uncle, and oppose not myself
            Against their will. – But who comes here?

                        Enter PERCY.

            Welcome, Harry. What, will not this castle yield?
PERCY   The castle royally is manned, my lord,   20
            Against thy entrance.
BULLING.   Royally?
            Why, it contains no king.
PERCY   Yes, my good lord,
            It doth contain a king. King Richard lies
            Within the limits of yon lime and stone,
            And with him are the Lord Aumerle, Lord Salisbury,
            Sir Stephen Scroope, besides a clergyman
            Of holy reverence; who, I cannot learn.
NORTH.   O, belike it is the Bishop of Carlisle.
BULLING.   [*to Northumberland:*] Noble lord,   30
            Go to the rude ribs of that ancient castle;
            Through brazen trumpet send the breath of parle
            Into his ruined ears, and thus deliver:
            Henry Bullingbrooke
            On both his knees doth kiss King Richard's hand,
            And sends allegiance and true faith of heart
            To his most royal person; hither come
            Even at his feet to lay my arms and power,
            Provided that my banishment repealed
            And lands restored again be freely granted.   40
            If not, I'll use th'advantage of my power,
            And lay the summer's dust with showers of blood,
            Rained from the wounds of slaughtered Englishmen,
            The which, how far off from the mind of Bullingbrooke
            It is such crimson tempest should bedrench
            The fresh green lap of fair King Richard's land,
            My stooping duty tenderly shall show.
            Go, signify as much, while here we march
            Upon the grassy carpet of this plain.
                            [*Northumberland and the trumpeter* 50
                                approach the castle walls.

Let's march without the noise of threat'ning drum,
That from this castle's tattered battlements
Our fair appointments may be well perused.
Methinks King Richard and myself should meet
With no less terror than the elements
Of fire and water, when their thund'ring shock
At meeting tears the cloudy cheeks of heaven.
Be he the fire, I'll be the yielding water;
The rage be his, whilst on the earth I rain
My waters: on the earth, and not on him.   60
March on, and mark King Richard how he looks.

*They march, then halt. Northumberland's trumpeter sounds a parle. A
trumpet within responds, and plays a flourish. Enter, on the walls,*
KING RICHARD, *the* BISHOP OF CARLISLE, AUMERLE,
SCROOPE *and* SALISBURY.

See, see, King Richard doth himself appear,
As doth the blushing discontented sun
From out the fiery portal of the east,
When he perceives the envious clouds are bent
To dim his glory and to stain the track
Of his bright passage to the occident.[61]

YORK   Yet looks he like a king: behold, his eye,
As bright as is the eagle's, lightens forth
Controlling majesty. Alack, alack, for woe,   70
That any harm should stain so fair a show!

RICHARD [*to Northumberland:*] We are amazed, and thus long
                                        have we stood
To watch the fearful bending of thy knee,
Because we thought ourself thy lawful king;
And if we be, how dare thy joints forget
To pay their aweful duty to our presence?
If we be not, show us the hand of God
That hath dismissed us from our stewardship;
For well we know, no hand of blood and bone
Can gripe the sacred handle of our sceptre,   80
Unless he do profane, steal, or usurp.
And though you think that all, as you have done,
Have torn their souls, by turning them from us,

And we are barren and bereft of friends,
Yet know, my master, God omnipotent,
Is mustering in his clouds, on our behalf,
Armies of pestilence, and they shall strike
Your children yet unborn and unbegot,
That lift your vassal hands against my head,
And threat the glory of my precious crown.   90
Tell Bullingbrooke, for yon methinks he stands,
That every stride he makes upon my land
Is dangerous treason: he is come to ope
The purple testament of bleeding war.[62]
But ere the crown he looks for live in peace,
Ten thousand bloody crowns of mothers' sons
Shall ill become the flower of England's face,
Change the complexion of her maid-pale peace
To scarlet indignation, and bedew
Her pastures' grass with faithful English blood.   100

NORTH.   The King of Heaven forbid, our lord the King
Should so with civil and uncivil arms
Be rushed upon! Thy thrice noble cousin,
Harry Bullingbrooke, doth humbly kiss thy hand,
And by the honourable tomb he swears,
That stands upon your royal grandsire's bones,
And by the royalties of both your bloods,
Currents that spring from one most gracious head,
And by the buried hand of warlike Gaunt,
And by the worth and honour of himself,   110
Comprising all that may be sworn or said:
His coming hither hath no further scope
Than for his lineal royalties, and to beg
Enfranchisement immediate on his knees;
Which on thy royal party granted once,
His glittering arms he will commend to rust,
His barbèd steeds to stables, and his heart
To faithful service of your Majesty.
This swears he, as he is a prince, is just;
And, as I am a gentleman, I credit him.   120

RICHARD   Northumberland, say thus the King returns:
His noble cousin is right welcome hither,

And all the number of his fair demands
Shall be accomplished without contradiction.
With all the gracious utterance thou hast,
Speak to his gentle hearing kind commends.
[*To Aumerle:*] We do debase ourself, cousin, do we not,
To look so poorly, and to speak so fair?
Shall we call back Northumberland, and send
Defiance to the traitor, and so die?   130

AUMERLE   No, good my lord; let's fight with gentle words,
Till time lend friends, and friends their helpful swords.

RICHARD   O God, O God, that e'er this tongue of mine,
That laid the sentence of dread banishment
On yon proud man, should take it off again
With words of sooth! O that I were as great
As is my grief, or lesser than my name!
Or that I could forget what I have been!
Or not remember what I must be now!
Swell'st thou, proud heart? I'll give thee scope to beat,   140
Since foes have scope to beat both thee and me.

AUMERLE   Northumberland comes back from Bullingbrooke.

RICHARD   [*To Northumberland:*] What must the King do now?
                                    Must he submit?
The King shall do it. Must he be deposed?
The King shall be contented. Must he lose
The name of King? A God's name let it go.
I'll give my jewels for a set of beads,
My gorgeous palace for a hermitage,
My gay apparel for an almsman's gown,
My figured goblets for a dish of wood,   150
My sceptre for a palmer's walking-staff,
My subjects for a pair of carvèd saints,
And my large kingdom for a little grave,
A little, little grave, an óbscure grave;
Or I'll be buried in the King's high-way,
Some way of common trade, where subjects' feet
May hourly trample on their Sovereign's head;
For on my heart they tread now whilst I live,
And buried once, why not upon my head?
– Aumerle, thou weep'st (my tender-hearted cousin).   160

We'll make foul weather with despisèd tears;
Our sighs and they shall lodge the summer corn,
And make a dearth in this revolting land.
Or shall we play the wantons with our woes,
And make some pretty match with shedding tears?
As thus: to drop them still upon one place,
Till they have fretted us a pair of graves
Within the earth; and therein laid: 'There lies
Two kinsmen digged their graves with weeping eyes.'
Would not this ill do well? – Well, well I see,   170
I talk but idly, and you laugh at me.
Most mighty prince, my Lord Northumberland,
What says King Bullingbrooke? Will his Majesty
Give Richard leave to live till Richard die?
You make a leg, and Bullingbrooke says 'Ay'.

NORTH. My lord, in the base court he doth attend,
To speak with you; may it please you to come down?

RICHARD Down, down I come, like glist'ring Phaeton,
Wanting the manage of unruly jades.[63]
'In the base court'? Base court, where kings grow base,   180
To come at traitors' calls, and do them grace.
'In the base court'? 'Come down'? Down court,
                                        down King!
For night-owls shriek where mounting larks should sing.
          [Exeunt, from above, King Richard and his associates.
                              Northumberland returns.

BULLING. What says his Majesty?

NORTH.   Sorrow and grief of heart
Makes him speak fondly, like a frantic man;
Yet he is come.

          Enter, below, KING RICHARD and his ASSOCIATES.

BULLING. Stand all apart,
And show fair duty to his Majesty.   [He kneels.
My gracious lord –

RICHARD Fair cousin, you debase your princely knee,   190
To make the base earth proud with kissing it.
Me rather had my heart might feel your love,
Than my unpleased eye see your courtesy.

Up, cousin, up; your heart is up, I know,
Thus high at least, [*He touches his crown.*]
                        although your knee be low.

BULLING. My gracious lord, I come but for mine own.

RICHARD   Your own is yours, and I am yours, and all.

BULLING. So far be mine, my most redoubted lord,
As my true service shall deserve your love.

RICHARD   Well you deserve: they well deserve to have,   200
That know the strong'st and surest way to get.
[*Bullingbrooke rises.*]
– Uncle, give me your hands; nay, dry your eyes:
Tears show their love, but want their remedies.
– Cousin, I am too young to be your father,
Though you are old enough to be my heir.
What you will have, I'll give, and willing too,
For do we must what force will have us do.
Set on towards London, cousin, is it so?

BULLING. Yea, my good lord.

RICHARD   Then I must not say 'No'.
                              [*Flourish. Exeunt.*]

SCENE 4.

In the Duke of York's garden.

Enter the QUEEN *and* TWO LADIES.

QUEEN   What sport shall we devise here in this garden,
To drive away the heavy thought of care?

LADY   Madam, we'll play at bowls.

QUEEN   'Twill make me think the world is full of rubs,
And that my fortune runs against the bias.

LADY   Madam, we'll dance.

QUEEN   My legs can keep no measure in delight,
When my poor heart no measure keeps in grief.[64]
Therefore, no dancing, girl; some other sport.

LADY   Madam, we'll tell tales.   10

QUEEN   Of sorrow or of joy?

LADY   Of either, madam.

QUEEN	Of neither, girl;
	For if of joy, being altogether wanting,
	It doth remember me the more of sorrow;
	Or if of grief, being altogether had,
	It adds more sorrow to my want of joy:
	For, what I have, I need not to repeat,
	And what I want, it boots not to complain.
LADY	Madam, I'll sing.
QUEEN	'Tis well that thou hast cause;
	But thou shouldst please me better, wouldst thou weep. 20
LADY	I could weep, madam, would it do you good.
QUEEN	And I could sing, would weeping do me good,
	And never borrow any tear of thee.⁶⁵

Enter a GARDENER *and* TWO SERVANTS.

But stay, here come the gardeners.
Let's step into the shadow of these trees.
My wretchedness unto a row of pins,
They will talk of state, for every one doth so
Against a change: woe is fore-run with woe.

[*The Queen and her ladies withdraw to eavesdrop.*

GARDENER	[*to one servant:*] Go, bind thou up young dangling
	apricocks,⁶⁶
	Which, like unruly children, make their sire 30
	Stoop with oppression of their prodigal weight.
	Give some supportance to the bending twigs.
	[*To the other:*] Go thou, and, like an executioner,
	Cut off the heads of too-fast-growing sprays
	That look too lofty in our commonwealth:
	All must be even in our government.
	You thus employed, I will go root away
	The noisome weeds which without profit suck
	The soil's fertility from wholesome flowers.
SERVANT	Why should we, in the compass of a pale, 40
	Keep law and form and due proportion,
	Showing as in a model our firm estate,
	When our sea-wallèd garden, the whole land,
	Is full of weeds, her fairest flowers choked up,
	Her fruit trees all unpruned, her hedges ruined,

Her knots disordered, and her wholesome herbs
Swarming with caterpillars?
GARDENER   Hold thy peace.
He that hath suffered this disordered spring
Hath now himself met with the fall of leaf.
The weeds which his broad-spreading leaves did shelter,   50
That seemed in eating him to hold him up,
Are plucked up root and all by Bullingbrooke:
I mean the Earl of Wiltshire, Bushy, Greene.
SERVANT   What, are they dead?
GARDENER   They are, and Bullingbrooke
Hath seized the wasteful King. O, what pity is it
That he had not so trimmed and dressed his land
As we this garden! We at time of year⁶⁷
Do wound the bark, the skin of our fruit trees,
Lest being over-proud in sap and blood,
With too much riches it confound itself.   60
Had he done so to great and growing men,
They might have lived to bear, and he to taste,
Their fruits of duty. Superfluous branches
We lop away, that bearing boughs may live:
Had he done so, himself had borne the crown,
Which waste of idle hours hath quite thrown down.
SERVANT   What? Think you the King shall be deposed?
GARDENER Depressed he is already, and deposed
'Tis doubt he will be. Letters came last night
To a dear friend of the good Duke of York's,   70
That tell black tidings.
QUEEN   O, I am pressed to death through want of speaking!
                                          [*She comes forward.*
Thou, old Adam's likeness, set to dress this garden,
How dares thy harsh rude tongue sound this
                                          unpleasing news?
What Eve, what serpent, hath suggested thee
To make a second Fall of cursèd man?
Why dost thou say King Richard is deposed?
Dar'st thou, thou little better thing than earth,
Divine his downfall? Say, where, when, and how,
Cam'st thou by these ill tidings? Speak, thou wretch!   80

GARDENER Pardon me, madam. Little joy have I
         To breathe this news, yet what I say is true.
         King Richard, he is in the mighty hold
         Of Bullingbrooke: their fortunes both are weighed.
         In your lord's scale is nothing but himself,
         And some few vanities that make him light;
         But in the balance of great Bullingbrooke,
         Besides himself, are all the English peers,
         And with that odds he weighs King Richard down.
         Post you to London, and you'll find it so;   90
         I speak no more than every one doth know.
QUEEN   Nimble Mischance, that art so light of foot,
         Doth not thy embassage belong to me,
         And am I last that knows it? O, thou think'st
         To serve me last, that I may longest keep
         Thy sorrow in my breast. – Come, ladies, go,
         To meet, at London, London's King in woe.
         What, was I born to this, that my sad look
         Should grace the triumph of great Bullingbrooke?
         Gardener, for telling me these news of woe,   100
         Pray God the plants thou graft'st may never grow.
                              [*Exeunt Queen and her ladies.*
GARDENER Poor Queen, so that thy state might be no worse,
         I would my skill were subject to thy curse.
         Here did she fall a tear: here in this place
         I'll set a bank of rue, sour herb of grace.
         Rue, even for ruth, here shortly shall be seen,
         In the remembrance of a weeping queen.   [*Exeunt.*

ACT 4, SCENE I.

London. Westminster Hall.

Enter, to Parliament, BULLINGBROOKE, AUMERLE, SURREY,
NORTHUMBERLAND, PERCY, FITZWATER *and other* LORDS;
the BISHOP OF CARLISLE *and the* ABBOT OF WESTMINSTER;
a HERALD *and* ATTENDANTS.

BULLING. Call forth Bagot.

Enter BAGOT, *guarded by* OFFICERS.

Now, Bagot, freely speak thy mind:
What thou dost know of noble Gloucester's death,
Who wrought it with the King, and who performed
The bloody office of his timeless end.

BAGOT Then set before my face the Lord Aumerle.

BULLING. – Cousin, stand forth, and look upon that man.

[Aumerle complies.

BAGOT My Lord Aumerle, I know your daring tongue
Scorns to unsay what once it hath delivered.
In that dead time when Gloucester's death was plotted, 10
I heard you say, 'Is not my arm of length,
That reacheth from the restful English court
As far as Callice, to mine uncle's head?'.
Amongst much other talk, that very time,
I heard you say that you had rather refuse
The offer of an hundred thousand crowns
Than Bullingbrooke's return to England;[68] adding
Withal, how blest this land would be, in this
Your cousin's death.

AUMERLE   Princes and noble lords,
What answer shall I make to this base man? 20
Shall I so much dishonour my fair stars,
On equal terms to give him chástisement?
Either I must, or have mine honour soiled
With the attainder of his sland'rous lips.

[He throws down his gage.

There is my gage, the manual seal of death,

That marks thee out for hell. I say thou liest,[69]
And will maintain what thou hast said is false
In thy heart-blood, though being all too base
To stain the temper of my knightly sword.

BULLING.   Bagot, forbear; thou shalt not take it up.   30

AUMERLE   Excepting one, I would he were the best
In all this presence that hath moved me so.

FITZWATER   If that thy valour stand on sympathy,
There is my gage, Aumerle, in gage to thine.[70]
                    [*He throws down his gage.*
By that fair sun which shows me where thou stand'st,
I heard thee say, and vauntingly thou spak'st it,
That thou wert cause of noble Gloucester's death.
If thou deniest it twenty times, thou liest,
And I will turn thy falsehood to thy heart,
Where it was forgèd, with my rapier's point.   40

AUMERLE   Thou dar'st not (coward) live to see that day.

FITZWATER   Now by my soul, I would it were this hour.

AUMERLE   Fitzwater, thou art damned to hell for this.

PERCY   Aumerle, thou liest: his honour is as true
In this appeal as thou art all unjust;
And that thou art so, there I throw my gage,
                    [*He throws down his gage.*
To prove it on thee to th'extremest point
Of mortal breathing. Seize it, if thou dar'st.

AUMERLE   And if I do not, may my hands rot off,
And never brandish more revengeful steel   50
Over the glittering helmet of my foe!

A LORD   I task the earth to the like (forsworn Aumerle),
And spur thee on with full as many 'Lies!'
As may be hollowed in thy treacherous ear
From sun to sun.[71] There is my honour's pawn;
                    [*He throws down his gage.*
Engage it to the trial if thou dar'st.

AUMERLE   Who sets me else? By heaven, I'll throw at all!
I have a thousand spirits in one breast,
To answer twenty thousand such as you.[72]

SURREY   My Lord Fitzwater, I do remember well   60
The very time Aumerle and you did talk.

FITZWATER 'Tis very true: you were in presence then,
         And you can witness with me this is true.
SURREY   As false, by heaven, as heaven itself is true.
FITZWATER Surrey, thou liest.
SURREY   Dishonourable boy!
         That lie shall lie so heavy on my sword,
         That it shall render vengeance and revenge,
         Till thou the lie-giver, and that lie, do lie
         In earth as quiet as thy father's skull.
         In proof whereof, there is my honour's pawn: 70
                              [*He throws down his gage.*
         Engage it to the trial if thou dar'st.
FITZWATER How fondly dost thou spur a forward horse!
         If I dare eat, or drink, or breathe, or live,
         I dare meet Surrey in a wilderness,
         And spit upon him, whilst I say he lies,
         And lies, and lies. There is my bond of faith,
         To tie thee to my strong correction.
                              [*He throws down his gage.*
         As I intend to thrive in this new world,
         Aumerle is guilty of my true appeal.
         Besides, I heard the banished Norfolk say   80
         That thou, Aumerle, didst send two of thy men
         To execute the noble Duke at Callice.
AUMERLE Some honest Christian trust me with a gage.
         That Norfolk lies. Here do I throw down this,
         If he may be repealed to try his honour.
                              [*He throws down a borrowed gage.*
BULLING. These differences shall all rest under gage
         Till Norfolk be repealed. Repealed he shall be,
         And, though mine enemy, restored again
         To all his lands and signories. When he's returned,
         Against Aumerle we will enforce his trial.   90
CARLISLE That honourable day shall ne'er be seen.
         Many a time hath banished Norfolk fought
         For Jesu Christ in glorious Christian field,
         Streaming the ensign of the Christian cross
         Against black pagans, Turks, and Saracens;
         And, toiled with works of war, retired himself

To Italy, and there at Venice gave
His body to that pleasant country's earth,
And his pure soul unto his captain, Christ,
Under whose colours he had fought so long.   100
BULLING. Why, Bishop, is Norfolk dead?
CARLISLE As surely as I live, my lord.
BULLING. Sweet peace conduct his sweet soul to the bosom
Of good old Abraham![73] Lords appellants,
Your differences shall all rest under gage,
Till we assign you to your days of trial.

Enter YORK.

YORK Great Duke of Lancaster, I come to thee
From plume-plucked Richard, who, with willing soul,
Adopts thee heir, and his high sceptre yields
To the possession of thy royal hand.   110
Ascend his throne, descending now from him,
And long live Henry, of that name the fourth![74]
BULLING. In God's name, I'll ascend the regal throne.
CARLISLE Marry, God forbid!
Worst in this royal presence may I speak,
Yet best beseeming me to speak the truth.[75]
Would God that any in this noble presence
Were enough noble to be upright judge
Of noble Richard. Then true noblesse would
Learn him forbearance from so foul a wrong.   120
What subject can give sentence on his King?
And who sits here that is not Richard's subject?
Thieves are not judged but they are by to hear,
Although apparent guilt be seen in them;
And shall the figure of God's majesty,
His captain, steward, deputy-elect,
Anointed, crownèd, planted many years,
Be judged by subject and inferior breath,
And he himself not present? O, forfend it, God,
That, in a Christian climate, souls refined   130
Should show so heinous, black, obscene a deed!
I speak to subjects, and a subject speaks,
Stirred up by God thus boldly for his King.

My Lord of Her'ford here, whom you call 'King',
Is a foul traitor to proud Her'ford's King;
And if you crown him, let me prophesy,
The blood of English shall manure the ground,
And future ages groan for this foul act;
Peace shall go sleep with Turks and infidels,
And, in this seat of peace, tumultuous wars   140
Shall kin with kin, and kind with kind, confound;
Disorder, horror, fear and mutiny
Shall here inhabit, and this land be called
'The field of Golgotha and dead men's skulls'.
O, if you raise this house against this house,
It will the woefullest division prove
That ever fell upon this cursèd earth.[76]
Prevent it, resist it, let it not be so,
Lest child, child's children, cry against you 'Woe!'.

NORTH.   Well have you argued, sir, and, for your pains,   150
Of capital treason we arrest you here:
– My Lord of Westminster, be it your charge
To keep him safely till his day of trial.
– May it please you, lords, to grant the Commons'
                                   suit?

BULLING.   Fetch hither Richard, that in common view
He may surrender; so we shall proceed
Without suspicion.

YORK   I will be his conduct.   [*Exit.*

BULLING.   Lords, you that here are under our arrest,
Procure your sureties for your days of answer.
Little are we beholding to your love,   160
And little looked for at your helping hands.

     Enter YORK *with* KING RICHARD. OFFICERS *follow, bearing*
                     the crown and sceptre.

RICHARD   Alack, why am I sent for to a king,
Before I have shook off the regal thoughts
Wherewith I reigned? I hardly yet have learned
To insinuate, flatter, bow, and bend my knee.
Give sorrow leave a while, to tutor me
To this submission. Yet I well remember

The favours of these men: were they not mine?
Did they not sometime cry 'All hail!' to me?
So Judas did to Christ:[77] but he, in twelve,   170
Found truth in all but one; I, in twelve
                                    thousand, none.
God save the King! Will no man say 'Amen'?
Am I both priest and clerk? Well then, 'Amen'.
God save the King, although I be not he;
And yet, 'Amen', if heaven do think him me.
To do what service am I sent for hither?

YORK   To do that office, of thine own good will,
Which tired majesty did make thee offer:
The resignation of thy state and crown
To Henry Bullingbrooke.   180

RICHARD   Give me the crown. – Here, cousin, seize the crown:
Here, cousin,
On this side, my hand, and on that side, thine.
Now is this golden crown like a deep well
That owes two buckets, filling one another,
The emptier ever dancing in the air,
The other down, unseen, and full of water:
That bucket down, and full of tears, am I,
Drinking my griefs, whilst you mount up on high.

BULLING.   I thought you had been willing to resign.   190

RICHARD   My crown I am, but still my griefs are mine:
You may my glories and my state depose,
But not my griefs; still am I king of those.

BULLING.   Part of your cares you give me with your crown.

RICHARD   Your cares set up do not pluck my cares down.
My care is loss of care, by old care done;
Your care is gain of care, by new care won:[78]
The cares I give, I have, though given away;
They 'tend the crown, yet still with me they stay.

BULLING.   Are you contented to resign the crown?   200

RICHARD   Ay, no; no, ay: for I must nothing be;
Therefore no 'no', for I resign to thee.[79]
Now, mark me how I will undo myself.
I give this heavy weight from off my head,
And this unwieldy sceptre from my hand,

The pride of kingly sway from out my heart;
With mine own tears I wash away my balm,
With mine own hands I give away my crown,
With mine own tongue deny my sacred state,
With mine own breath release all duteous oaths.   210
All pomp and majesty I do forswear;
My manors, rents, revénues, I forgo;
My acts, decrees and statutes, I deny.
God pardon all oaths that are broke to me;
God keep all vows unbroke are made to thee.
Make me, that nothing have, with nothing grieved,
And thou with all pleased, that hast all achieved.
Long mayst thou live in Richard's seat to sit,
And soon lie Richard in an earthy pit.
'God save King Henry', un-kinged Richard says,   220
'And send him many years of sunshine days.'
– What more remains?

NORTH.   [*proffering papers:*]   No more, but that you read
These accusations and these grievous crimes,
Committed by your person and your followers
Against the state and profit of this land;
That, by confessing them, the souls of men
May deem that you are worthily deposed.

RICHARD   Must I do so? And must I ravel out
My weaved-up follies? Gentle Northumberland,
If thy offences were upon recórd,   230
Would it not shame thee, in so fair a troop
To read a lecture of them? If thou wouldst,
There shouldst thou find one heinous article,
Containing the deposing of a king
And cracking the strong warrant of an oath,
Marked with a blot, damned in the book of heaven.
– Nay, all of you, that stand and look upon me,
Whilst that my wretchedness doth bait myself,
Though some of you, with Pilate, wash your hands,
Showing an outward pity; yet you Pilates   240
Have here delivered me to my sour cross,
And water cannot wash away your sin.[80]

NORTH.   My lord, dispatch: read o'er these articles.

RICHARD Mine eyes are full of tears; I cannot see;
And yet salt water blinds them not so much,
But they can see a sort of traitors here.
Nay, if I turn mine eyes upon myself,
I find myself a traitor with the rest;
For I have given here my soul's consent
T'undeck the pompous body of a king;   250
Made glory base, a sovereignty a slave,
Proud majesty a subject, state a peasant.

NORTH. My lord —

RICHARD No lord of thine, thou haught-insulting man;
Nor no man's lord. I have no name, no title,
No, not that name was given me at the font,
But 'tis usurped. Alack the heavy day,
That I have worn so many winters out,
And know not now what name to call myself![81]
O, that I were a mockery-king of snow,   260
Standing before the sun of Bullingbrooke,
To melt myself away in water-drops!
Good King, great King, and yet not greatly good,
And if my word be sterling yet in England,
Let it command a mirror hither straight,
That it may show me what a face I have,
Since it is bankrupt of his majesty.

BULLING. Go some of you, and fetch a looking-glass.
                        [*Exeunt two attendants.*

NORTH. Read o'er this paper while the glass doth come.

RICHARD Fiend, thou torments me ere I come to hell.   270

BULLING. Urge it no more, my Lord Northumberland.

NORTH. The Commons will not then be satisfied.

RICHARD They shall be satisfied: I'll read enough,
When I do see the very book indeed
Where all my sins are writ, and that's myself.

                Enter an ATTENDANT *with a mirror.*

Give me that glass, and therein will I read.
                        [*He studies his reflection.*
No deeper wrinkles yet? Hath sorrow struck
So many blows upon this face of mine,

And made no deeper wounds? O flatt'ring glass,
Like to my followers in prosperity, 280
Thou dost beguile me. Was this face the face
That every day, under his household roof,
Did keep ten thousand men?[82] Was this the face
That like the sun did make beholders wink?
Was this the face that faced so many follies,
And was at last out-faced by Bullingbrooke?
A brittle glory shineth in this face;
As brittle as the glory is the face –
                    [*He hurls the mirror down, smashing it.*
For there it is, cracked in an hundred shivers.
Mark, silent King, the moral of this sport: 290
How soon my sorrow hath destroyed my face.

BULLING. The shadow of your sorrow hath destroyed
The shadow of your face.

RICHARD   Say that again.
The 'shadow' of my sorrow: ha, let's see:
'Tis very true, my grief lies all within,
And these external manners of laments
Are merely shadows to the unseen grief
That swells with silence in the tortured soul.
There lies the substance; and I thank thee, King,
For thy great bounty, that not only giv'st 300
Me cause to wail, but teachest me the way
How to lament the cause. I'll beg one boon,
And then be gone, and trouble you no more.
Shall I obtain it?

BULLING.   Name it, fair cousin.

RICHARD 'Fair cousin'? I am greater than a king;
For when I was a king, my flatterers
Were then but subjects; being now a subject,
I have a king here to my flatterer.
Being so great, I have no need to beg.

BULLING. Yet ask. 310

RICHARD And shall I have?

BULLING. You shall.

RICHARD Then give me leave to go.

BULLING. Whither?

RICHARD   Whither you will, so I were from your sights.
BULLING.   Go, some of you, convey him to the Tower.
RICHARD   O good: 'convey'! Conveyers are you all,
          That rise thus nimbly by a true king's fall.

                              [*Exit Richard, guarded.*[83]

BULLING.   On Wednesday next, we solemnly set down
          Our coronation: lords, prepare yourselves.   320

Exeunt all except ABBOT OF WESTMINSTER, CARLISLE *and* AUMERLE.

ABBOT   A woeful pageant have we here beheld.
CARLISLE The woe's to come: the children yet unborn
          Shall feel this day as sharp to them as thorn.
AUMERLE   You holy clergymen, is there no plot
          To rid the realm of this pernicious blot?
ABBOT   My lord,
          Before I freely speak my mind herein,
          You shall not only take the Sacrament
          To bury mine intents, but also to effect
          Whatever I shall happen to devise.[84]   330
          I see your brows are full of discontent,
          Your hearts of sorrow, and your eyes of tears.
          Come home with me to supper; I will lay
          A plot shall show us all a merry day.   [*Exeunt.*

ACT 5, SCENE I.

London. A street leading to the Tower.

Enter the QUEEN *with her* ATTENDANTS.

QUEEN
This way the King will come: this is the way
To Julius Cæsar's ill-erected tower,[85]
To whose flint bosom my condemnèd lord
Is doomed a prisoner by proud Bullingbrooke.
Here let us rest, if this rebellious earth
Have any resting for her true King's Queen.

Enter RICHARD *with* GUARDS.

But soft, but see, or rather do not see,
My fair rose wither. Yet look up, behold,
That you in pity may dissolve to dew,
And wash him fresh again with true-love tears.   10
– Ah, thou, the model where old Troy did stand!
Thou map of honour, thou King Richard's tomb,
And not King Richard; thou most beauteous inn,
Why should hard-favoured grief be lodged in thee,
When triumph is become an alehouse guest?[86]

RICHARD
Join not with grief, fair woman, do not so,
To make my end too sudden. Learn, good soul,
To think our former state a happy dream,
From which awaked, the truth of what we are
Shows us but this: I am sworn brother (sweet)   20
To grim Necessity, and he and I
Will keep a league till death. Hie thee to France,
And cloister thee in some religious house.
Our holy lives must win a new world's crown,
Which our profane hours here have stricken down.[87]

QUEEN
What, is my Richard both in shape and mind
Transformed and weakened? Hath Bullingbrooke
                                        deposed
Thine intellect? Hath he been in thy heart?
The lion, dying, thrusteth forth his paw,
And wounds the earth, if nothing else, with rage   30

To be o'erpow'red; and wilt thou pupil-like
Take the correction, mildly kiss the rod,
And fawn on rage with base humility,
Which art a lion and the king of beasts?

RICHARD   A king 'of beasts', indeed; if aught but beasts,
I had been still a happy king of men.
Good sometime Queen, prepare thee hence for France.
Think I am dead, and that even here thou tak'st,
As from my death-bed, thy last living leave.
In winter's tedious nights sit by the fire   40
With good old folks, and let them tell thee tales
Of woeful ages long ago betid;
And ere thou bid good night, to quit their griefs,
Tell thou the lamentable tale of me,[88]
And send the hearers weeping to their beds;
For why, the senseless brands will sympathise
The heavy accent of thy moving tongue,
And in compassion weep the fire out,
And some will mourn in ashes, some coal-black,
For the deposing of a rightful king.   50

Enter NORTHUMBERLAND.

NORTH.   My lord, the mind of Bullingbrooke is changed:
You must to Pomfret, not unto the Tower.
And, madam, there is order tane for you:
With all swift speed, you must away to France.

RICHARD   Northumberland, thou ladder wherewithal
The mounting Bullingbrooke ascends my throne,
The time shall not be many hours of age
More than it is, ere foul sin, gathering head,
Shall break into corruption. Thou shalt think,
Though he divide the realm and give thee half,   60
It is too little, helping him to all.
He shall think that thou, which know'st the way
To plant unrightful kings, wilt know again,
Being ne'er so little urged another way,
To pluck him headlong from the úsurped throne.
The love of wicked men converts to fear,
That fear to hate, and hate turns one or both

To worthy danger and deservèd death.

NORTH.   My guilt be on my head, and there an end.

Take leave and part, for you must part forthwith.   70

RICHARD   Doubly divorced? Bad men, you violate
A twofold marriage: 'twixt my crown and me,
And then betwixt me and my married wife.
[*To her:*] Let me unkiss the oath 'twixt thee and me;
And yet not so, for with a kiss 'twas made.
– Part us, Northumberland: I towards the north,
Where shivering cold and sickness pines the clime;
My wife to France, from whence, set forth in pomp,
She came adornèd hither like sweet May,
Sent back like Hallowmas or short'st of day.[89]   80

QUEEN   And must we be divided? Must we part?

RICHARD   Ay, hand from hand (my love) and heart from heart.

QUEEN   – Banish us both, and send the King with me.

NORTH.   That were some love, but little policy.

QUEEN   Then whither he goes, thither let me go.

RICHARD   So two, together weeping, make one woe.
Weep thou for me in France, I for thee here;
Better far off than, near, be ne'er the nea'r.[90]
Go, count thy way with sighs, I mine with groans.

QUEEN   So longest way shall have the longest moans.   90

RICHARD   Twice for one step I'll groan, the way being short,
And piece the way out with a heavy heart.
Come, come, in wooing sorrow let's be brief,
Since, wedding it, there is such length in grief.
One kiss shall stop our mouths, and dumbly part;
Thus give I mine, and thus take I thy heart. [*They kiss.*

QUEEN   Give me mine own again: 'twere no good part
To take on me to keep and kill thy heart.   [*They kiss.*
So, now I have mine own again, be gone,
That I may strive to kill it with a groan.   100

RICHARD   We make woe wanton with this fond delay.
Once more, adieu; the rest, let sorrow say.

[*Exeunt Richard, guards and Northunberland.*
Exeunt, in a different direction, the Queen
and her attendants.

SCENE 2.

Inside the Duke of York's house.

Enter the DUKE *and* DUCHESS OF YORK.

DUCHESS My lord, you told me you would tell the rest,
When weeping made you break the story off,
Of our two cousins' coming into London.

YORK Where did I leave?

DUCHESS   At that sad stop, my lord,
Where rude misgoverned hands, from windows' tops,
Threw dust and rubbish on King Richard's head.

YORK Then, as I said, the Duke, great Bullingbrooke,
Mounted upon a hot and fiery steed,
Which his aspiring rider seemed to know,
With slow but stately pace kept on his course,   10
Whilst all tongues cried 'God save thee, Bullingbrooke!'.
You would have thought the very windows spake,
So many greedy looks of young and old
Through casements darted their desiring eyes
Upon his visage, and that all the walls
With painted imagery had said at once
'Jesu preserve thee! Welcome, Bullingbrooke!'
Whilst he, from one side to the other turning,
Bareheaded, lower than his proud steed's neck,
Bespake them thus: 'I thank you, countrymen.';   20
And thus still doing, thus he passed along.

DUCHESS Alack, poor Richard! Where rode he the whilst?

YORK As, in a theatre, the eyes of men,
After a well-graced actor leaves the stage,
Are idly bent on him that enters next,
Thinking his prattle to be tedious,
Even so, or with much more contempt, men's eyes
Did scowl on Richard.[91] No man cried, 'God save him!',
No joyful tongue gave him his welcome home;
But dust was thrown upon his sacred head,   30
Which with such gentle sorrow he shook off,
His face still cómbating with tears and smiles

(The badges of his grief and patience),
That had not God for some strong purpose steeled
The hearts of men, they must perforce have melted,
And barbarism itself have pitied him.
But heaven hath a hand in these events,
To whose high will we bound our calm conténts.
To Bullingbrooke are we sworn subjects now,
Whose state and honour I for aye allow.   40

Enter AUMERLE.

DUCHESS Here comes my son, Aumerle.
YORK   Aumerle that was,
But that is lost for being Richard's friend;
And, madam, you must call him 'Rutland' now.[92]
I am in Parliament pledge for his truth
And lasting fealty to the new-made King.
DUCHESS – Welcome, my son. Who are the violets now,
That strew the green lap of the new-come spring?
AUMERLE Madam, I know not, nor I greatly care not.
God knows I had as lief be none as one.
YORK Well, bear you well in this new spring of time, 50
Lest you be cropped before you come to prime.
What news from Oxford? Hold these jousts and
             triumphs?[93]
AUMERLE For aught I know, my lord, they do.
YORK You will be there, I know.
AUMERLE If God prevent not, I purpose so.
YORK What seal is that, that hangs without thy bosom?
Yea, look'st thou pale? Let me see the writing.
AUMERLE My lord, 'tis nothing.
YORK   No matter then who see it.
I will be satisfied: let me see the writing.
AUMERLE I do beseech your Grace to pardon me; 60
It is a matter of small consequence,
Which for some reasons I would not have seen.
YORK Which for some reasons, sir, I mean to see:
I fear, I fear.
DUCHESS   What should you fear?
'Tis nothing but some bond that he is entered into

For gay apparel 'gainst the triumph day.

YORK Bound to himself? What doth he with a bond
That he is bound to? Wife, thou art a fool.⁹⁴
— Boy, let me see the writing.

AUMERLE I do beseech you, pardon me; I may not show it.   70

YORK I will be satisfied; let me see it, I say.
          [*He plucks it out of his bosom and reads it.*⁹⁵
Treason, foul treason! Villain, traitor, slave!

DUCHESS What is the matter, my lord?

YORK [*calling:*] Ho! Who is within there? Saddle my horse.
God for his mercy! What treachery is here!

DUCHESS Why, what is it, my lord?

YORK Give me my boots, I say; saddle my horse.
— Now by mine honour, by my life, by my troth,
I will appeach the villain.

DUCHESS   What is the matter?

YORK Peace, foolish woman.   80

DUCHESS I will not 'peace'. — What is the matter, Aumerle?

AUMERLE Good mother, be content; it is no more
Than my poor life must answer.

DUCHESS   Thy life answer?

YORK [*calling:*] Bring me my boots, I will unto the king.

          Enter York's servant with boots.

DUCHESS Strike him, Aumerle! Poor boy, thou art amazed.
          [*She pushes the servant aside.*
— Hence, villain! Never more come in my sight.

YORK Give me my boots, I say.

DUCHESS Why, York, what wilt thou do?
Wilt thou not hide the trespass of thine own?
Have we more sons? Or are we like to have?⁹⁶   90
Is not my teeming date drunk up with time?
And wilt thou pluck my fair son from mine age,
And rob me of a happy mother's name?
Is he not like thee? Is he not thine own?

YORK Thou fond mad woman,
Wilt thou conceal this dark conspiracy?
A dozen of them here have tane the Sacrament,
And interchangeably set down their hands

	To kill the King at Oxford.
DUCHESS	He shall be none.
	We'll keep him here, then what is that to him? 100
YORK	Away, fond woman! Were he twenty times my son,
	I would appeach him.
DUCHESS	Hadst thou groaned for him
	As I have done, thou wouldst be more pitiful.
	But now I know thy mind: thou dost suspect
	That I have been disloyal to thy bed,
	And that he is a bastard, not thy son.
	Sweet York, sweet husband, be not of that mind:
	He is as like thee as a man may be,
	Not like to me or any of my kin,
	And yet I love him.
YORK	Make way, unruly woman. 110

        [Exeunt York and the servant.

DUCHESS After, Aumerle! Mount thee upon his horse,
    Spur post, and get before him to the King,
    And beg thy pardon ere he do accuse thee.
    I'll not be long behind: though I be old,
    I doubt not but to ride as fast as York;
    And never will I rise up from the ground,
    Till Bullingbrooke have pardoned thee. Away, be gone!

            [Exeunt rapidly.

SCENE 3.

Inside Windsor Castle.

Enter KING HENRY *(formerly Bullingbrooke),* PERCY *and other* LORDS.

HENRY Can no man tell me of my unthrifty son?
    'Tis full three months since I did see him last.
    If any plague hang over us, 'tis he.
    I would to God, my lords, he might be found:
    Inquire at London, 'mongst the taverns there,
    For there, they say, he daily doth frequent
    With unrestrainèd loose companions,
    Even such, they say, as stand in narrow lanes,

And beat our watch, and rob our passengers,
While he, young wanton and effeminate boy,⁹⁷   10
Takes on the point of honour to support
So dissolute a crew.

PERCY   My lord, some two days since, I saw the Prince,
And told him of those triumphs held at Oxford.

HENRY   And what said the gallant?

PERCY   His answer was, he would unto the stews,
And from the common'st creature pluck a glove,
And wear it as a favour, and with that
He would unhorse the lustiest challenger.

HENRY   As dissolute as desperate; yet through both   20
I see some sparks of better hope, which elder years
May happily bring forth. – But who comes here?

                    Enter AUMERLE.

AUMERLE   Where is the King?

HENRY   What means our cousin, that he stares and looks
So wildly?

AUMERLE   God save your Grace, I do beseech your Majesty,
To have some conference with your Grace alone.

HENRY   – Withdraw yourselves, and leave us here alone.
                    [*Exeunt all except Henry and Aumerle.*
           –What is the matter with our cousin now?

AUMERLE   [*kneeling:*] For ever may my knees grow to the earth,   30
My tongue cleave to my roof within my mouth,
Unless a pardon ere I rise or speak.

HENRY   Intended, or committed, was this fault?
If on the first, how heinous e'er it be,
To win thy after-love, I pardon thee.

AUMERLE   [*rising:*] Then give me leave that I may turn the key,
That no man enter till my tale be done.

HENRY   Have thy desire. [*Aumerle locks the door. Knocking heard.*

YORK   [*beyond the door:*] My liege, beware, look to thyself!
Thou hast a traitor in thy presence there.   40

HENRY   [*drawing his sword:*] Villain, I'll make thee safe.

AUMERLE   Stay thy revengeful hand; thou hast no cause to fear.

YORK   Open the door, secure foolhardy King!
Shall I for love speak treason to thy face?
Open the door, or I will break it open!

King Henry opens the door, admits YORK, *and locks it again.*

HENRY   What is the matter, uncle? Speak.
          Recover breath. Tell us how near is danger,
          That we may arm us to encounter it.

YORK   Peruse this writing here, and thou shalt know
          The treason that my haste forbids me show.   50
                                    [*He delivers the document.*

AUMERLE   Remember, as thou read'st, thy promise past.
          I do repent me; read not my name there;
          My heart is not confederate with my hand.

YORK   It was (villain), ere thy hand did set it down.
          – I tore it from the traitor's bosom, King.
          Fear, and not love, begets his penitence:
          Forget to pity him, lest thy pity prove
          A serpent that will sting thee to the heart.

HENRY   O heinous, strong and bold conspiracy!
          – O loyal father of a treacherous son!   60
          Thou sheer, immaculate and silver fountain,
          From whence this stream, through muddy passages,
          Hath held his current, and defiled himself!
          Thy overflow of good converts to bad;
          And thy abundant goodness shall excuse
          This deadly blot in thy digressing son.

YORK   So shall my virtue be his vice's bawd,
          And he shall spend mine honour with his shame,
          As thriftless sons their scraping fathers' gold:
          Mine honour lives when his dishonour dies,   70
          Or my shamed life in his dishonour lies.
          Thou kill'st me in his life: giving him breath,
          The traitor lives, the true man's put to death.

DUCHESS   [*beyond:*] What ho, my liege! For God's sake, let
                                                    me in!

HENRY   What shrill-voiced suppliant makes this eager cry?

DUCHESS   A woman, and thy aunt, great King; 'tis I.
          Speak with me, pity me, open the door;
          A beggar begs that never begged before.

HENRY   Our scene is altered from a serious thing,
          And now changed to 'The Beggar and the King'.⁹⁸   80
          – My dangerous cousin, let your mother in;

	I know she is come to pray for your foul sin.
YORK	If thou do pardon whosoever pray,
	More sins for this forgiveness prosper may.
	This festered joint cut off, the rest rest sound;
	This, let alone, will all the rest confound.

[Aumerle unlocks the door.

Enter the DUCHESS.

DUCHESS	O King, believe not this hard-hearted man!
	Love loving not itself, none other can.[99]
YORK	Thou frantic woman, what dost thou make here?
	Shall thy old dugs once more a traitor rear? 90
DUCHESS	Sweet York, be patient. – Hear me, gentle liege.

[She kneels.

HENRY	Rise up, good aunt.
DUCHESS	Not yet, I thee beseech.
	For ever will I walk upon my knees,
	And never see day that the happy sees,
	Till thou give joy, until thou bid me joy,
	By pardoning Rutland, my transgressing boy.
AUMERLE	*[kneeling:]* Unto my mother's prayers I bend my knee.
YORK	*[kneeling:]* Against them both, my true joints bended be.
	Ill mayst thou thrive, if thou grant any grace.[100]
DUCHESS	Pleads he in earnest? Look upon his face: 100
	His eyes do drop no tears, his prayers are in jest;
	His words come from his mouth, ours from our breast.
	He prays but faintly, and would be denied;
	We pray with heart and soul, and all beside.
	His weary joints would gladly rise, I know;
	Our knees shall kneel till to the ground they grow.
	His prayers are full of false hypocrisy;
	Ours of true zeal and deep integrity.
	Our prayers do out-pray his; then let them have
	That mercy which true prayer ought to have. 110
HENRY	Good aunt, stand up.
DUCHESS	Nay, do not say 'stand up';
	Say 'pardon' first, and afterwards 'stand up'.
	And if I were thy nurse, thy tongue to teach,
	'Pardon' should be the first word of thy speech.
	I never longed to hear a word till now;

Say 'pardon', King; let pity teach thee how.
The word is short, but not so short as sweet,
No word like 'pardon' for kings' mouths so meet.
YORK   Speak it in French, King, say 'pardonnez-moy'.[101]
DUCHESS   Dost thou teach pardon pardon to destroy?   120
Ah, my sour husband, my hard-hearted lord,
That sets the word itself against the word!
[*To King:*] Speak 'pardon' as 'tis current in our land;
The chopping French we do not understand.
Thine eye begins to speak: set thy tongue there;
Or in thy piteous heart plant thou thine ear,
That hearing how our plaints and prayers do pierce,
Pity may move thee 'pardon' to rehearse.
HENRY   Good aunt, stand up.
DUCHESS   I do not sue to stand.
Pardon is all the suit I have in hand.   130
HENRY   I pardon him, as God shall pardon me.
DUCHESS   O happy vantage of a kneeling knee!
Yet am I sick for fear: speak it again.
Twice saying 'pardon' doth not pardon twain,
But makes one pardon strong.
HENRY   I pardon him
With all my heart.[102]
DUCHESS   A god on earth thou art.
HENRY   But, for our trusty brother-in-law and the abbot,
With all the rest of that consorted crew,
Destruction straight shall dog them at the heels.
– Good uncle, help to order several powers   140
To Oxford, or where'er these traitors are.
They shall not live within this world, I swear,
But I will have them, if I once know where.
Uncle, farewell, and cousin, adieu:
Your mother well hath prayed, and prove you true.
DUCHESS   Come, my old son; I pray God make thee new.
                  [*Exeunt, Kimg Henry separately.*

SCENE 4.

Inside Windsor Castle.

Enter SIR PIERCE OF EXTON *and* SERVANTS.

EXTON   Didst thou not mark the King, what words he spake?
        'Have I no friend will rid me of this living fear?':
        Was it not so?
SERVANT   These were his very words.
EXTON   'Have I no friend?', quoth he. He spake it twice,
        And urged it twice together, did he not?
SERVANT   He did.
EXTON   And, speaking it, he wishtly looked on me,
        As who should say, 'I would thou wert the man
        That would divorce this terror from my heart',
        Meaning the King at Pomfret. Come, let's go: 10
        I am the King's friend, and will rid his foe.   [*Exeunt.*

SCENE 5.

In the prison of Pomfret Castle.

Enter RICHARD.

RICHARD   I have been studying how I may compare
        This prison where I live unto the world;
        And for because the world is populous,
        And here is not a creature but myself,
        I cannot do it; yet I'll hammer't out.
        My brain I'll prove the female to my soul,
        My soul the father, and these two beget
        A generation of still-breeding thoughts;
        And these same thoughts people this little world
        In humours like the people of this world,   10
        For no thought is contented. The better sort,
        As thoughts of things divine, are intermixed
        With scruples, and do set the word itself
        Against the word,[103]
        As thus: 'Come, little ones'; and then again,

'It is as hard to come, as for a camel
To thread the postern of a small needle's eye'.[104]
Thoughts tending to ambition, they do plot
Unlikely wonders: how these vain weak nails
May tear a passage through the flinty ribs　　　　　　20
Of this hard world, my raggèd prison walls;
And, for they cannot, die in their own pride.
Thoughts tending to content flatter themselves
That they are not the first of Fortune's slaves,
Nor shall not be the last; like silly beggars
Who, sitting in the stocks, refuge their shame,
That many have and others must sit there;
And in this thought they find a kind of ease,
Bearing their own misfortunes on the back
Of such as have before endured the like.　　　　　　30
Thus play I in one person many people,
And none contented. Sometimes am I king;
Then treasons make me wish myself a beggar,
And so I am. Then crushing penury
Persuades me I was better when a king;
Then am I kinged again, and by and by
Think that I am un-kinged by Bullingbrooke,
And straight am nothing. But whate'er I be,
Nor I, nor any man that but man is,
With nothing shall be pleased, till he be eased　　　40
With being nothing.　　　　　　　　　[*Music plays.*
　　　　　　Music do I hear?
Ha ha! Keep time! How sour sweet music is,
When time is broke and no proportion kept.
So is it in the music of men's lives;
And here have I the daintiness of ear
To check time broke in a disordered string,
But, for the concord of my state and time,
Had not an ear to hear my true time broke.
I wasted time, and now doth Time waste me;
For now hath Time made me his numb'ring clock:　　50
My thoughts are minutes, and with sighs they jar
Their watches on unto mine eyes, the outward watch,
Whereto my finger, like a dial's point,

Is pointing still, in cleansing them from tears.[105]
Now, sir, the sound that tells what hour it is
Are clamorous groans which strike upon my heart,
Which is the bell. So sighs, and tears, and groans,
Show minutes, times, and hours; but my time
Runs posting on in Bullingbrooke's proud joy,
While I stand fooling here, his Jack o'th'clock.   60
This music mads me; let it sound no more,
For though it have holp madmen to their wits,
In me, it seems, it will make wise men mad.
Yet blessing on his heart that gives it me,
For 'tis a sign of love; and love to Richard
Is a strange brooch in this all-hating world.

Enter a GROOM.

GROOM   Hail, royal Prince!
RICHARD   Thanks, noble peer;
The cheapest of us is ten groats too dear.[106]
What art thou? And how comest thou hither,
Where no man never comes but that sad dog   70
That brings me food to make misfortune live?
GROOM   I was a poor groom of thy stable, King,
When thou wert King; who, travelling towards York,
With much ado at length have gotten leave
To look upon my sometimes royal master's face.
O, how it erned my heart, when I beheld
In London streets that coronation day,
When Bullingbrooke rode on roan Barbary,
That horse that thou so often hast bestrid,
That horse that I so carefully have dressed.   80
RICHARD   Rode he on Barbary? Tell me, gentle friend,
How went he under him?
GROOM   So proudly as if he disdained the ground.
RICHARD   So proud that Bullingbrooke was on his back.
That jade hath ate bread from my royal hand;
This hand hath made him proud with clapping him.
Would he not stumble? Would he not fall down
(Since pride must have a fall), and break the neck
Of that proud man that did usurp his back?[107]
– Forgiveness, horse! Why do I rail on thee,   90

Since thou, created to be awed by man,
Wast born to bear? I was not made a horse,
And yet I bear a burthen like an ass,
Spurred, galled and tired by jauncing Bullingbrooke.

Enter KEEPER, *bearing food.*

KEEPER   [*to the groom:*] Fellow, give place: here is no longer stay.
RICHARD   [*to the groom:*] If thou love me, 'tis time thou wert away.
GROOM   What my tongue dares not, that my heart shall say.
                                                    [*Exit.*
KEEPER   [*putting down the food:*] My lord, will't please you to
                                                    fall to?
RICHARD   Taste of it first, as thou art wont to do.[108]
KEEPER   My lord, I dare not. Sir Pierce of Exton, who lately   100
            came from the King, commands the contrary.
RICHARD   The devil take Henry of Lancaster, and thee!
            Patience is stale, and I am weary of it.
                                        [*He strikes the keeper.*
KEEPER   Help, help, help!

EXTON *and several armed* SERVANTS *rush in. They attack Richard.*

RICHARD   How now? What means Death in this rude assault?
                [*He snatches a weapon from a servant, and kills him.*
            Villain, thy own hand yields thy death's instrument.
                                            [*He kills another.*
            Go thou, and fill another room in hell.
                                        [*Exton strikes him down.*
            That hand shall burn in never-quenching fire
            That staggers thus my person: Exton, thy fierce hand
            Hath with the King's blood stained the King's own land.   110
            – Mount, mount, my soul; thy seat is up on high,
            Whilst my gross flesh sinks downward, here to die.
                                                    [*He dies.*

EXTON   As full of valour as of royal blood:
            Both have I spilt. O, would the deed were good!
            For now the devil that told me I did well
            Says that this deed is chronicled in hell.
            This dead King to the living King I'll bear.
            Take hence the rest, and give them burial here.
                                    [*Exeunt, carrying the bodies.*

SCENE 6.

Inside Windsor Castle.

Flourish. Enter KING HENRY, *the* DUKE OF YORK,
LORDS *and* ATTENDANTS.

HENRY   Kind uncle York, the latest news we hear
             Is that the rebels have consumed with fire
             Our town of Ciceter in Gloucestershire;
             But whether they be tane or slain, we hear not.

Enter NORTHUMBERLAND.

             – Welcome, my lord: what is the news?
NORTH.   First, to thy sacred state wish I all happiness.
             The next news is, I have to London sent
             The heads of Salisbury, Spencer, Blunt and Kent.
             The manner of their taking may appear
             At large discoursèd in this paper here.   [*He presents it.*   10
HENRY   We thank thee, gentle Percy, for thy pains,
             And to thy worth will add right worthy gains.

Enter FITZWATER.

FITZWATER   My lord, I have from Oxford sent to London
             The heads of Broccas and Sir Benet Seely,
             Two of the dangerous consorted traitors
             That sought at Oxford thy dire overthrow.
HENRY   Thy pains, Fitzwater, shall not be forgot;
             Right noble is thy merit, well I wot.

Enter PERCY *with the* BISHOP OF CARLISLE.

PERCY   The grand conspirator, Abbot of Westminster,
             With clog of conscience and sour melancholy   20
             Hath yielded up his body to the grave;
             But here is Carlisle living, to abide
             Thy kingly doom and sentence of his pride.
HENRY   Carlisle, this is your doom:
             Choose out some secret place, some reverend room,
             More than thou hast, and with it joy thy life;
             So as thou liv'st in peace, die free from strife;
             For though mine enemy thou hast ever been,
             High sparks of honour in thee have I seen.

Enter EXTON *with* SERVANTS *who bear a coffin.*

EXTON   Great King, within this coffin I present
        Thy buried fear: herein all breathless lies   30
        The mightiest of thy greatest enemies,
        Richard of Bordeaux, by me hither brought.
HENRY   Exton, I thank thee not, for thou hast wrought
        A deed of slander, with thy fatal hand,
        Upon my head and all this famous land.
EXTON   From your own mouth, my lord, did I this deed.
HENRY   They love not poison that do poison need,
        Nor do I thee: though I did wish him dead,
        I hate the murtherer, love him murtherèd.
        The guilt of conscience take thou for thy labour,   40
        But neither my good word nor princely favour.
        With Cain go wander through the shades of night,
        And never show thy head by day nor light.[109]
                              [*Exeunt Exton and the servants.*
        – Lords, I protest, my soul is full of woe,
        That blood should sprinkle me to make me grow.
        Come, mourn with me for what I do lament,
        And put on sullen black incontinent.
        I'll make a voyage to the Holy Land,
        To wash this blood off from my guilty hand.
        March sadly after, grace my mournings here,   50
        In weeping after this untimely bier.
                              [*Exeunt with the coffin.*

                    FINIS.

In these notes, the abbreviations include the following:

Cf., cf.:   *confer* (Latin): compare;

e.g.:   *exempli gratia* (Latin): for example;

F1:   the First Folio (1623);

F2:   the Second Folio (1632);

Holinshed: Raphael Holinshed and others: *Chronicles*, Vol. III
(2nd edn.; London: 1587);

Q: Quarto;

Q1:   the First Quarto (1597);

S.D.:   stage-direction.

Biblical quotations are from the Bishops' Bible: *The Holy Bible*
(London: Richarde Jugge, 1573). When quoting this Bible and
Holinshed, I modernise the spelling and punctuation.

In the case of a pun, a metaphor or an ambiguity, the meanings
may be distinguished as (a) and (b), or as (a), (b) and (c).

1 (Title) *RICHARD II*:   In Q1, the full title is: 'THE Tragedie
of King Richard the second.'; but F1 gives: 'The life and death
of King Richard the Second.'

2 (1.1.40) *Too . . . so,*:   'so nobly-born that you should never be
like that'.

3 (1.1.67–8) *let this . . . lie.*:   His 'this' may refer to his sword or
to the allegation in line 68.

4 (1.1.69) gage::   A gage thrown down is a material token of a
challenge to a fight. The person who picks it up thereby accepts
the challenge, although it may later be thrown back down to
convert the acceptance to a rejection. The gage is probably a
glove or gauntlet, as is implied at 4.1.25 by the phrase 'manual

seal of death'. On various occasions (e.g. pp. 491, 493, 512),
Holinshed specifies sometimes gloves and sometimes hoods.

5 (1.1.95) *all . . . years*:   since the Peasants' Revolt of 1381.

6 (1.1.100–108) *That he . . . spent.*:   According to Holinshed
(p. 489), Thomas Woodstock, the Duke of Gloucester, was
murdered at Calais (probably by suffocation, not by blood-
shed,) while in Mowbray's custody. The chronicler says that
the murder was vengefully instigated by the King, encouraged
by Aumerle. Mowbray procrastinated, being reluctant to kill
the Duke (hence 'Neglected my sworn duty', line 134), but
Richard sent word that Mowbray would be killed if he failed to
act quickly. Mowbray's servants then murdered the captive.
(Woodstock was Bullingbrooke's uncle.) In lines 104–5,
Bullingbrooke recalls Genesis, Chap. 4, which tells how Cain
slew his brother, Abel, because God had accepted Abel's
sacrifice but not Cain's. God said to the killer: '[The] voice of
thy brother's blood cryeth unto me out of the ground.' (4:10.)

7 (1.1.130) *Upon . . . account,*:   'for the balance of a large sum,'.

8 (1.1.135–41) *For you . . . it.*:   Holinshed (p. 494) reports
Mowbray's statement that he had once sought to ambush and
slay Gaunt, but had subsequently been pardoned by him.

9 (1.1.153) *Let's . . . blood.*:   'let's eliminate this wrath without
losing blood.' Blood-letting was a surgical procedure then
regarded as therapeutic. (As line 157 shows, physicians consulted almanacs to find the favourable months for such surgery.
Where Q1 has 'month', F1 has 'time'.)

10 (1.1.172–3) *his . . . poison.*:   'the heart's blood of him who
uttered this venomous slander.'

11 (1.1.174–6) *lions . . . gage.*:   Lions were depicted in the King's
coat of arms (but a lion was also part of Mowbray's). By 'spots',
Mowbray refers both to the proverbially unchangeable markings
of the leopard (see Jeremiah 13:23) and to the stains of slander.

12 (1.1.203) *design . . . chivalry.*:   'designate the winner in knightly
combat.'

13 (1.2.1) *the . . . blood*:   Gaunt was Woodstock's elder brother.
They were two of the seven sons of Edward III.

14 (1.2.7) *Who . . . earth,*:   Occasionally, as here and at 5.5.58,
'hours' is metrically disyllabic; so are 'fire' and 'fires' at 1.3.294,
2.1.34 and 5.1.48, and 'tired' at 4.1.178.

15 (1.3.84) *Mine . . . thrive!*:   To repair the pentameter, some
editors emend Q1's and F1's 'innocence' as 'innocency'; but a
lengthened 'George' suffices.

16 (1.3.134–8) *And . . . sleep*::   These lines are present in Q1 but
absent from F1. In Q1 they precede the present lines 129–33,
leading to obvious inconsistency in the sense. My transposition
of them reduces the inconsistency. Perhaps 129–33 and 134–8
were originally alternatives.

17 (1.3.181) *(Our . . . ourselves)*:   '(your allegiance to me being
cancelled during your exile)'.

18 (1.3.202) *My . . . life,*:   God declared: 'He that overcometh
shall be thus clothed in white array, and I will not blot out his
name out of the book of life . . . ' (Revelation 3:5). The 'book
of life' is the list of people selected for immortality in Heaven.

19 (1.3.224) *blindfold . . . son.*:   Atropos, one of the three classical
Fates, cuts the thread of each person's life. She is sometimes
deemed blind or blindfold.

20 (1.3.239–42) *O . . . destroyed.*:   These lines are present in Q1
but absent from F1.

21 (1.3.249–50) *What . . . show.*:   'Send to me in writing, from
your foreign residence, what I must not learn from you directly
(as you are banished).'

22 (1.3.268–93) *Nay . . . light.*:   This passage is present in Q1 but
absent from F1.

23 (1.4.20) *He . . . cousin,*:   Richard, Bullingbrooke and Aumerle
were first cousins, sons of three brothers.

24 (1.4.23) *Ourself . . . Greene*:   Q1 has: 'Our selfe and Bushie,'.
Q6 (1634) has: 'Our selfe, and *Bushy*, *Bagot* here and *Greene*'.
F1 has: 'Our selfe, and *Bushy*: heere *Bagot* and *Greene*'.

25 (1.4.45–52) *We . . . presently.*:   Richard (here as often elsewhere) uses the royal plural. To 'farm' the realm is to sell to
various lords the right to collect the profits from royal taxes.
(Holinshed, p. 496, reports the belief that 'the king had set to
farm the realm of England'.) The 'blank charters' resemble
blank cheques. To prove their loyalty, subjects deemed
prosperous are obliged to sign undertakings to pay money to
the King's agents, the sum being stipulated by the agent. The
anonymous play *Woodstock* shows in detail this unpopular
mode of taxation.

26 (2.1.18) *As . . . fond;*:   This is my emendation of Q1's 'As
   praises of whose taste the wise are found'. F1 has 'As praises of
   his state: then there are sound'.

27 (2.1.53–6) *Renownèd . . . son*::   Gaunt recalls such crusader-
   kings as Edward I and Richard I. The term 'ransom' echoes the
   Bible: Jesus said that he came 'to give his life a ransom for
   many' (Matthew 20:28; Mark 10:45); St. Paul says that Jesus
   was 'a ransom for all' (1 Timothy 2:5–6).

28 (2.1.70) *being . . . more.*:   Q1 has 'being ragde, do rage the
   more.', and F1 has 'being rag'd, do rage the more.'. Editors
   emend the line in various ways. My emendation uses the verb
   'rag', meaning 'gall, fret'.

29 (2.1.86) *Since . . . me,*:   'because you seek to ensure that my
   lineage ends with me (by exiling my son),'. (Actually, Gaunt
   had four sons.)

30 (2.1.94) *Ill . . . ill.*:   'seeing you with the (impaired) sight of a
   sick man, and seeing that you, being morally ill, are of ill
   repute.'

31 (2.1.98–9) *Commit'st . . . thee.*:   The term 'anointed' suggests
   both the anointing of the King at his coronation and the
   treating of a sick man's body with ointments. The 'physicians'
   are probably Richard's flattering associates.

32 (2.1.115–19) *And . . . residence.*:   At the present line 115, Q1
   has 'And thou' followed by the King's 'A lunatike leane-witted
   foole,', but F1 has 'And————' followed by the King's 'And
   thou, a lunaticke leane-witted foole,'. At the present line 117,
   Q1 has 'Darest', which may be pronounced with one or two
   syllables; F1, which is frequently more sensitive to the metre,
   has 'Dar'st', implying that the 'tion' of 'admonition' is
   pronounced disyllabically to regularise the line's pentameter.
   In lines 116–19, Richard means that Gaunt, exploiting the fact
   that he has a chilly ailment, is offering a cold rebuke, which
   accordingly inflicts on Richard's cheeks a pallor, angrily chasing
   the royal blood from its natural place.

33 (2.1.124–7) *O . . . caroused.*:   'You, son of my brother (Edward,
   the Black Prince): do not spare me because I am the son of his
   father (Edward III). You are like the pelican's offspring, which
   (according to legend) nourish themselves by drinking the
   parent's blood. The blood of our family has already been

tapped by you for drunken carousals.' (He recalls that Richard is guilty of killing Woodstock and seizing his estate.)

34 (2.1.143–6) *He . . . is*.:   York says that Gaunt loves Richard as much as he loves his son, but the King wilfully misconstrues York to mean that Gaunt has as little love for Richard as his son has; so 'my feelings are the same as theirs, and nothing changes'.

35 (2.1.156–8) *those . . . live*.: 'those shaggy-haired Irish foot-soldiers, who survive like privileged poisonous snakes (in a land from which St. Patrick is supposed to have banished all snakes).'

36 (2.1.167–70) *Nor . . . face*.: Holinshed (p. 495) reports that Bullingbrooke, during his exile in France, planned marriage to the French King's cousin, but Richard intervened to prevent the match. The anonymous play *Woodstock* says (unhistorically) that Richard disgraced York and banished him from the court, which may explain York's reference (in line 168) to a 'disgrace'. The phrase 'bend one wrinkle on' means 'direct one frown against'.

37 (2.1.202–4) *Call . . . homage,*:   'revoke the official documents which allowed him, through his legal representatives, to claim his inheritance, and deny him the opportunity of swearing allegiance to the monarch (in response to the ratified claim),'. This closely follows a passage in Holinshed, p. 496.

38 (2.1.253–4) *But . . . blows*.:   In 1398 Richard had ceded Brest (a town in western France) to the Duke of Brittany.

39 (2.1.280) *Thomas . . . heir,*:   This is an editorial emendation, replacing an evidently missing (and possibly censored) line. The person who 'broke from the Duke of Exeter' was, according to Holinshed, not Cobham but the Earl of Arundel's son. (Holinshed, pp. 496 and 498.) In 1595, another Earl of Arundel (a Catholic) was executed. Line 282's 'His brother' means 'The Earl of Arundel's brother'.

40 (2.2.18) *pérspectives,*:   The term 'perspective' referred to numerous kinds of optically-deceptive representations. Here the reference is to a picture behind multifaceted glass. Observed frontally ('rightly'), the image is confusingly multiplied; observed obliquely or from the side ('awry'), it is clarified. At lines 20–24, Bushy then contradicts himself in saying that by looking wrongly ('awry') on the King's departure, the Queen sees more to lament than she would if she looked correctly on it, seeing it 'as it is'.

41 (2.2.25) *More than . . . seen,*:   In this line, Q1 has 'more is'; but
F1 (as usual, more responsive to metre) has 'more's', thus
regularising the line as another of the occasional hexameters
(alexandrines) in the play.

42 (2.2.30–40) *so . . . wot.*:   'so grievously sad that, although I
think I am thinking of nothing, I am obliged to feel faint and to
recoil from that oppressive vacancy.' Bushy then says that this is
mere fancy. She replies that it is not in the least like fancy.
Fanciful grief is engendered by some real grief, but hers is
begotten by nothing, or else something has the absent thing
which causes her grief. What she has is hers 'by reversion': it
will pass to her when its present owner relinquishes it. She
knows only as nameless woe what she does not yet fully know
and cannot name. (In line 31, F1 has 'As though' where Q1 has
'As thought'.)

43 (2.2.88) *The nobles . . . cold,*:   This hexametrical line corres-
ponds to Q1 and F1. Some editors convert it to pentameter,
thus: 'The nobles they are fled, the commons cold,'. Several of
York's subsequent lines, including 90 and 103, read (or may be
read) as hexameters.

44 (2.2.105) *sister . . . me.*:   Subconscious thoughts of his sister-
in-law (the deceased Duchess) lead him to address his niece
mistakenly as 'sister'. The term 'cousin' could mean 'kins-
woman' and refer to various relationships.

45 (2.2.116–121) *Well . . . seven.*:   Editors lineate this passage in
various ways to reduce its metrical irregularity, but a degree of
irregularity tallies with York's sense that all is left 'At six and
seven'. Where Q1 has 'Barkly', F1 mends the metre with
'Barkley Castle'.

46 (2.3.70) *my answer . . . 'Lancaster',*:   'I answer only to the name
of "Lancaster",'. (He refers to the Duchy of Lancaster, of
which he had been deprived by Richard.)

47 (2.4.8–9) *The bay-trees . . . heaven;*:   Holinshed (p. 496) says that
previously, throughout England, 'old bay trees withered' (but
'grew green again'). Samuel Daniel's *First Fowre Books* (1595,
Vol. I, stanzas 114–15,) says that portentous meteors were seen.

48 (3.1.11–13) *You . . . bed,*:   This allegation of homosexuality
appears to be unhistorical, though Holinshed (p. 508) declares
the King guilty of 'abominable adultery'.

49 (3.2.1) *Barkloughly . . . hand?*: A version of 'Barclowlie',
Holinshed's error for 'Hertlowli', a name of the modern
Harlech (in northern Wales).

50 (3.2.29–32) *The means . . . redress.*: These lines are present in
Q1 but absent from F1. The words 'neglected; else, if ' emend
metrically Q1's 'neglected. Else'.

51 (3.2.40) *In . . . here;*: Q1 has: 'In murthers and in outrage
bouldy here,'; F1 has: 'In Murthers and in Out-rage bloody
here:'.

52 (3.2.49) *Whilst . . . Antipodes,*: 'while I [like the sun] was
roaming among the people who live on the opposite side of the
earth,'. (Richard thus refers to the Irish.) This line is present in
Q1 but absent from F1.

53 (3.2.55) *Can . . . king.*: By changing Q1's 'off from' to 'from',
F1 corrects the line and improves the metre.

54 (3.2.85) *Is . . . names?*: I follow Q1's figure here. F1 musters
'fortie thousand' names.

55 (3.2.102) *Cry . . . decay?*: Where Q1 has 'ruine, and', F1 has
'Ruine, Losse,'.

56 (3.2.116–19) *Thy very . . . seat:*; Beadsmen (often elderly)
were men hired to pray for the souls of other people, notably
their benefactors. Yew-trees (often grown in grave-yards) are
doubly fatal because their foliage and berries are poisonous
and their wood is used to make bows. Distaff-women are,
literally, spinsters: they hold the pole bearing the flax or wool
to be spun. A 'bill' is a pole topped with a metal blade.

57 (3.2.132–4) *Three . . . offence!*: Judas betrayed Jesus. Richard
refers to three Judases rather than to four, suggesting that here
Shakespeare may think that the Earl of Wiltshire (Scroope) is
Bagot; but in Act 4, scene 1, Bagot reappears. The present lines
133–4 appear thus in Q1: 'Would they make peace? terrible
hel, / Make war vpon their spotted soules for this.'; but F1,
improving the metre, gives: 'Would they make peace? terrible
Hell make warre / Vpon their spotted Soules for this Offence.'

58 (3.2.153–4) *that . . . bones.*: Editors speculate that the 'small
model' may be: (a) the curving grave-mound; (b) an effigy of
the dead person; (c) the corpse's body. The first option seems
preferable, as the phrase 'paste and cover' recalls the curving
pastry-covering of a pasty.

59 (3.2.183–5) *Fear . . . breath*.: 'If you are frightened and are slain, nothing can be worse. If (in contrast) you fight with determination and are slain, in such a death you vanquish Death's power; whereas to fear dying is to offer servile tribute to Death.' (I emend the punctuation of Q1 and F1, notably in changing 'come to fight,' to 'come. To fight'.)

60 (3.2.203) *party*.:   Q1 has 'partie.' (i.e. 'side.'); F1 has 'Faction.'.

61 (3.3.62–7) *See . . . occident*.:   An image of the sun was one of Richard's heraldic emblems.

62 (3.3.91–4) *Tell . . . war*.:   In line 91, 'stands' follows Q1; F1 has 'is'. In 93, 'ope' follows the more metrical F1; Q1 has 'open'. 'The purple testament of bleeding war' is war's will, written in blood, bequeathing slaughter.

63 (3.3.178–9) *Down . . . jades*.:   'Phaeton' is trisyllabic: 'Fáy-ee-tòn'. Phaeton, son of Helios (or Apollo), the sun-god, attempted to drive the chariot of the sun, but was unable to control the horses. To save the earth from being burned, Zeus slew Phaeton.

64 (3.4.4–8) *'Twill . . . grief*.:   In bowls, a 'rub' is an obstacle, and a 'bias' is a lead weight to make the bowl run a curving course. Lines 7 and 8 wittily exploit the ambiguity of 'measure' ('dance-step', 'moderation',) and mean: 'My legs can take no pleasure in a dance-step, when my unfortunate heart knows no moderation in its grief.'

65 (3.4.22–3) *And . . . thee*.:   'And, if weeping made me feel better, I would sing [for joy], and would not need you to supply me with tears.'

66 (3.4.29) *Go . . . apricocks*,:   Here 'young' is an emendation. Q1 has 'yong', later quartos have 'yon', and F1 has 'yond'; but 'young' matches the 'children' of the next line.

67 (3.4.54–7) *They . . . year*.   Q1 has: 'They are. / And Bulling-brooke hath ceasde the wastefull king, / Oh what pitie is it that he had not so trimde / And drest his land as we this garden at time of year'. F1, apart from minor variations (e.g. 'seiz'd' and 'King' for 'ceasde' and 'king'), is the same. The phrase 'at time of year' means 'in season'.

68 (4.1.17) *Than . . . England*;:   'than accept Bullingbrooke's return to England;'. As was made obvious in Act I, scene I, Gloucester was killed before Bullingbrooke's exile; so here either Bagot lies or Shakespeare errs.

69 (4.1.26) *That . . . liest,*:   'I say', present in Q1, is absent from
F1.

70 (4.1.31–4) *Excepting . . . thine.*:   Aumerle means: 'I wish that
the person who made me so angry were the best nobleman in
this entire assembly (apart from Bullingbrooke, of course).'
Fitzwater replies: 'If you really wish to challenge someone as
high in rank as yourself, there is my gage, to rival yours.'

71 (4.1.52–5) *I task . . . sun.*:   'Aumerle, you liar, I make the
ground bear a similar gage, and I incite you by yelling in your
ear the word "Lies!" as often as may be done between sunrise
and sunset.'

72 (4.1.52–9) *I task . . . you.*:   These lines, present in Q1, are
absent from F1.

73 (4.1.103–4) *Sweet . . . Abraham!*:   'And it came to pass, that the
beggar [Lazarus] died, and was carried by the angels into
Abraham's bosom . . . ' (Luke 16:22). Abraham was the biblical
patriarch; to be 'carried to his bosom' is to be transported to
heaven.

74 (4.1.112) *And . . . fourth!*:   Q1 has 'And long liue Henry fourth
of that name.' F1 has 'And long liue *Henry*, of that Name the
Fourth.'

75 (4.1.115–16) *Worst . . . truth.*:   'In the presence of this [newly-
declared] royal person, I may be the least worthy to speak; but
yet it is most appropriate for me [being a clergyman] to declare
the truth.'

76 (4.1.144–7) *The . . . earth.*:   Mark 15:22 says that Jesus was
brought to be crucified at 'a place named Golgotha, which is,
if a man interpret it, a place of a skull'. So here 'the field of
Golgotha' probably means 'the place of suffering and death'.
Carlisle proceeds to prophesy the warfare between the Houses
of York and Lancaster, and perhaps recalls the Biblical
warning that a house divided against itself cannot continue
(Mark 3:25).

77 (4.1.169–70) *Did . . . Christ:*:   According to Matthew 26:49,
Judas said 'Hail master' when betraying Jesus. Subsequently
Jesus was treated as a 'mockery-king' before being killed.

78 (4.1.195–7) *Your . . . won:*:   'Your newly-established respon-
sibilities do not reduce my sorrows. My sorrow is for loss of

responsibility, a loss caused by a previous worry (the rebellion) which is now ended. Your worry is the acquisition of responsibility which you have effected by new effort.'

79 (4.1.201–2) *Ay . . . thee.*:   'Yes, no; and I? No. No, I must say "Yes" - and there can be no "I", for I must be nothing; and therefore I cannot say "no", for I submit to you (and resign my office to you).' (Richard also puns on 'no' and 'know'.)

80 (4.1.239–42) *Though . . . sin.*:   After questioning Jesus, Pontius Pilate washed his hands to demonstrate that he disclaimed responsibility for Jesus's death, which was demanded by the Jews ('all the people'). (Cf. Bullingbrooke's words at 3.1.5–6 and 5.6.50.) Pilate nevertheless sent Jesus to the soldiers to be crucified. Richard says that his own cross (his impending suffering) is 'sour' (bitter), perhaps recalling the 'vinegar . . . mingled with gall' and the sponge of vinegar given to Christ. (Matthew 27:24–50.)

81 (4.1.255–9) *I have . . . myself!*:   French chroniclers reported a legend that Richard was not the true son of the Black Prince but the illegitimate son a of priest of Bordeaux, his original Christian name being 'Jehan' (i.e. 'John').

82 (4.1.281–3) *Was . . . men?*:   Cf. Christopher Marlowe's *Dr Faustus*: 'Was this the face that launched a thousand ships . . . ?'.

83 (4.1.154–318) - *May . . . guarded.*:   This long passage, absent from Q1, Q2 and Q3 (having, almost certainly, been censored), appears in Q4, later quartos and F1.

84 (4.1.328–30) *You . . . devise.*:   'you shall swear by the Eucharist not only to conceal my purposes but also to undertake whatever plan I shall happen to devise.'

85 (5.1.2) *To . . . tower,*:   The Tower of London was built by William the Conqueror on the site of Roman fortifications supposed to have been established by Julius Cæsar. It is here termed 'ill-erected' because it will confine Richard and perhaps because numerous prisoners had suffered and died there.

86 (5.1.11–15) – *Ah . . . guest?*:   To her, Richard is the pattern of fallen greatness, like the ground-plan of ruined Troy. He is like a map showing where honour once resided, or a tomb of the true King Richard. He resembles a beautiful inn (or mansion) which must accommodate ugly grief, whereas

Bullingbrooke resembles a mere alehouse which yet accommodates triumph.

87 (5.1.24–5) *Our . . . down.*:   'We must live holy lives in order to win a new crown in heaven, to replace the crown which was struck down by sinful hours on this earth.' See 2 Timothy 4:8. (F1 has 'stricken downe' where Q1 has 'throwne downe'.)

88 (5.1.44) *Tell . . . me,*:   Where Q1 has 'tale', F1 has 'fall': either is good.

89 (5.1.80) *Sent . . . day.*:   Hallowmas, the Feast of All Hallows (All Saints) is on November 1st. The shortest day is the winter solstice, on or near December 22nd.

90 (5.1.88) *Better . . . nea'r.*:   'It's better for you to be far away than to be near but never near enough [for us to be together].' (Here, 'nea'r' implies 'nearer, near enough'.)

91 (5.2.28) *Did . . . Richard.*:   Q1 had 'Did scowle on gentle Ric.', but this 'gentle' is probably an error resulting from the compositor's sighting of 'gentle' in line 31. F1, rectifying the metre, omits 'gentle' and thus reduces the line from an alexandrine to a pentameter; though, either way, it has a feminine ending. (Later, at line 81, where Q1 has 'Aumerle', F1 has 'Sonne', which makes a smoother but less colloquial line.)

92 (5.2.43) *you . . . now.*:   Aumerle, deprived of his ducal title, remained Earl of Rutland. (For clarity, I retain 'Aumerle' as his speech-prefix.)

93 (5.2.52) *What . . . triumphs?*:   Q1 has: 'What newes from Oxford, do these iusts & triumphs hold?'. F1 has: 'What newes from Oxford? Holds these Iusts & Triumphs?'. (In other words: 'What's the news from Oxford? Will those jousts and processions still take place?'.)

94 (5.2.67–8) *Bound . . . fool.*:   If Aumerle had signed a bond to borrow money, the bond would be held by the creditor.

95 (5.2, S.D. after 71) *He . . . it.*:   I follow Q1's S.D.: '*He pluckes it out of his bosome and reades it.*'. F1 has: '*Snatches it*'.

96 (5.2.90) *Have . . . have?*:   This Duchess (the Duke of York's second wife) was actually the stepmother of Aumerle, who had a brother and a sister.

97 (5.3.9–10) *beat . . . boy,*:   'beat our watchmen and rob the pedestrians, while he, dissolute youth and self-indulgent boy,'. ('While' is an emendation of Q1's and F1's 'Which'.)

98   (5.3.80) *'The . . . King'*.:   Scholars, unable to identify a play
      with such a title, suggest that Bullingbrooke may be recalling
      the ballad sometimes entitled 'King Cophetua and the Beggar-
      Maid'.

99   (5.3.88) *Love . . . can*.:   'If a person [such as York] has no love
      for his own flesh and blood [Aumerle], he can have no love
      for anyone else [- even the King].'

100   (5.3.99) *Ill . . . grace*.:   This line (which maintains the rhyme-
      scheme) is present in Q1 but absent from F1.

101   (5.3.119) *'pardonnez-moy'*.:   'excuse me', a courteous refusal.
      The French pronunciation is Anglicised: 'moy' rhymes with
      'destroy'.

102   (5.3.135–6) *I . . . heart*.:   I follow Q1 and F1. Some editors
      regularise the rhyme-pattern by re-arranging the words as:
      'With all my heart / I pardon him.'.

103   (5.5.13–14) *the word . . . word,*:   Q1 has: 'the word it selfe /
      Against the word,'; whereas F1 has: 'the Faith it selfe /
      Against the Faith:'.

104   (5.5.15–17) *As . . . eye'*.:   Jesus's welcome to children (in
      Matthew 19:14, Mark 10:14 and Luke18:16) can be interpreted
      to mean that salvation is readily available, but his reference to
      the eye of a needle (in Matthew 19:24, Mark 10:25 and Luke
      18:25) suggests that salvation may elude the rich.

105   (5.5.47–54) *But . . . tears*.:   'but, where the harmony of my
      royal condition and times were concerned, I lacked awareness
      that I was not maintaining order. I wasted time, and now
      Time lays me waste; for now Time has made me into his
      clock that numbers the hours and minutes. My thoughts are
      the minutes, and, with sighs for ticks, their vigils are recorded
      on my eyes, the lookouts and clock-face, at which my finger,
      like the hand on a dial, constantly points, as it cleans away the
      tears.' (At line 58, 'times' may mean the quarter- or half-
      hours, which some clocks indicated by bell-notes.)

106   (5.5.68) *The . . . dear*.:   One coin, a 'royal', was worth ten
      shillings; another, a 'noble', was worth six shillings and eight
      pence. The difference in price is 'ten groats': forty pence.
      Richard says that the groom, in calling him 'royal', has
      overpriced the cheaper of the two men, the prisoner; so they
      are both equal.

107 (5.5.87–9) *Would . . . back?*:   'Pride must have a fall' is proverbial, deriving from Proverbs 16:18.

108 (5.5.99) *Taste . . . do.*:   Such tasting would reduce the risk of poisoning.

109 (5.6.43–4) *With . . . light.*:   After Cain slew Abel, God said: 'And now art thou cursed from the earth . . . A fugitive and a vagabond shalt thou be in the earth.' (Genesis 4:11–12.)

GLOSSARY

Where a pun, a metaphor or an ambiguity occurs, the meanings are distinguished as (a) and (b), or (a), (b) and (c), etc. Otherwise, alternative meanings are distinguished as (i) and (ii), or as (i), (ii) and (iii), etc. Abbreviations include the following: adj., adjective; adv., adverb; e.g., for example; etc., and so on; fig., figuratively; interj., interjection; It., Italian; lit., literally; n., noun; S.D., stage-direction; vb., verb.

a: **a God's name**: in God's name; **John a Gaunt**: John of Gaunt.

abide: endure.

Abraham: biblical patriarch.

absent: **absent time**: period of royal absence.

abuse (vb.): wrong.

accomplished: equipped.

accuse my zeal: impugn my ardour.

advisèd: deliberate; intentional.

affect (n.): affection.

afore: before.

against: 3.4.28: in anticipation of.

aggravate the note: emphasise the disgrace.

ague: fever with shivering spells; **ague-fit**: shivering-fit.

alarms: **home alarms**: domestic disputes.

all-amiss: utterly-wrongly.

amazed: (i: 3.3.72:) astounded; (ii: 5.2.85: a) bewildered;

(b) distraught.

amazing: stupefying.

ancient: (i: 1.1.9:) long-established; (ii: 2.1.248:) bygone.

anointed: 2.1.98: (a) anointed as King; (b) treated with ointments.

answer: (i: 1.1.38, 198: a) pay for; (b) give account of; (ii: 1.1.80:) respond to.

antic (n.): 3.2.162: (a) jester; (b) grotesque figure.

apparent: evident; obvious.

appeach: accuse; lay evidence against.

appeal (n.): 1.1.4; 4.1.45, 79: (a) impeachment for treason; (b) challenge to trial by combat.

appeal (vb.): 1.1.9, 27, 142; 1.3.21: (a) impeach for treason; (b) formally accuse and challenge.

appellant (n.): challenger.

appellant (adj.): accusing.

appointment: equipment.

apprehension: awareness.
approve: prove.
apricock: apricot.
arbitrate: resolve; decide.
argument: topic.
arms: armour.
as: 1.3.55: insofar as.
aspéct: (i: 1.3.127:) spectacle;
  (ii: 1.3.209): appearance.
atone: reconcile.
attach: arrest.
attainder: allegation.
attending: awaiting.
attorney-general: leading law-
  officer.
awe (n.): 1.1.118: awe-inspiring
  power.
aweful: awe-filled.
awry: 2.2.19: (a) obliquely;
  (b) wrongly.
aye: 5.2.40: ever.

baffle: affront.
bait (vb.): torment.
balm: (i: 1.1.172:) ointment;
  (ii: 3.2.55; 4.1.207:) sacred oil
  for coronations.
band: bond.
barbèd: armoured.
Barkloughly: (error for)
  Hertlowli: Harlech.
barren: (i: 1.3.168:) vacant;
  (ii: 3.2.153:) bare; (iii: 3.3.84:)
  deprived.
base: (i: 3.3.176, 180:) lower;
  (ii: 3.3.180, 182: a) lower;
  (b) despicable.
bawd: pimp.
bay (n.): 2.3.127: last stand.
beads: **set of beads**: rosary.
beadsman: person hired to pray.

beguile: wile away.
benevolence: forced loan.
Berkeley Castle: castle in
  Gloucestershire.
beshrew: curse.
betid: happened.
betimes: soon.
better other's: 1.1.22: exceed
  the previous day's.
bias: **against the bias**: askew.
bill: blade-topped pole.
blank (n.): **blank charter**:
  document used for extortion.
blaze: outburst.
bleed: 1.1.157: draw blood.
boisterous: violent.
bonnet: cap.
boot (n.): 1.1.164: profit.
boot (vb.): avail.
bound (vb): (i: 1.2.58:) rebound;
  (ii: 5.2.38:) limit; (iii: 5.2.67,
  68:) obligated; **bound in**:
  (i: 2.1.61:) surrounded;
  (ii: 2.1.63:) overcome.
boy: 4.1.65: (a) wretch;
  (b) upstart.
brace (n.): pair.
brand: ember.
braving: defiant.
breath: 3.2.164: brief time.
breathe: 1.1.173; 1.3.257;
  3.4.82: utter.
breed: (i: 2.1.45:) race;
  (ii: 2.1.52:) lineage.
bring: 1.3.304: accompany.
Bristow: Bristol.
Brittaine: Brittany.
broken: 2.1.257: financially
  ruined.
broking pawn: being a pledge
  in a pawnshop.

brook (vb.): 3.2.2: (a) rate; (b) like.

burthenous: burdensome.

business: 2.2.75: (a) matter; (b) activity.

but: 4.1.122: except when; **but now**: 3.2.76: just now.

buzz (vb.): 2.1.26: whisper busily.

by: 2.1.52: on account of.

Cain: biblical slayer of his brother.

caitiff (adj.): wretched.

Callice: Calais.

care: (i: 2.2.79: a) woe; (b) worry; (ii: 3.4.2:) woe; (iii: 4.1.195-7: a) grief; (b) worry; (c) responsibility.

career: encounter.

careful: worrying.

care-tuned: attuned to woe.

casement: hinged window.

casque: helmet.

caterpillar (fig.): parasite.

Caucasus: mountain-range between Black Sea and Caspian Sea.

challenge law: demand my rights.

change: 3.2.189: exchange.

check (vb.): rebuke.

choler: 1.1.153: (a) anger; (b) bile.

chopping: 5.3.124: equivocating.

Ciceter: Cirencester, Glos.

civil: of the same country.

clap: (i: 3.2.114:) confine; (ii: 5.5.86:) pat.

clean (adv.): 3.1.10: utterly.

clerk: priest's helper who utters responses.

climate, clime: region.

clog (n.): guilty weight; **clogging**: impeding.

close (n.): 2.1.12: musical conclusion.

coat: (i: 1.3.75; 1.4.61:) armour; (ii: 3.1.24:) coat of arms.

colours: 3.2, S.D.; 3.3, S.D.: (a) flags; (b) standards.

comfortable: comforting.

commends (n.): greetings; compliments.

commons: ordinary folk; **Commons**: House of Commons.

compassionate: 1.3.174: (a) displaying sorrow; (b) eliciting pity.

compass of a pale: fenced area.

complain: bewail; **complain myself**: utter my lamentations.

complotted: conspired.

composition: physical state.

conceit: (i: 2.2.33: a) fancy; (b) fantasy; (ii: 2.2.34:) imagined grief; (iii: 3.2.166:) pride.

conclude: come to terms.

condition: (i: 2.3.106:) personal quality; (ii: 2.3.107): state; situation.

confines (n.): territories.

confound: destroy.

conjuration: **senseless conjuration**: 3.2.23: (a) injunction to the insentient; (b) inane invocation.

consent . . . to: 1.2.25-6: abet.

consorted: complicit.

convert (vb.): undergo a change.

convey: (i: 2.1.137; 4.1.316:)
  conduct; (ii: 4.1.317:
  (a) conduct; (b) steal.

conveyer: 4.1.317:
  (a) transferor; (b) thief.

cormorant: voracious sea-bird.

corruption: 5.1.59: (a) foul
  matter from a boil;
  (b) rebellion.

Cotshall: the Cotswold Hills.

couch: lodge.

court: 3.3.176, 180, 182:
  courtyard.

cover . . . heads: replace . . .
  hats.

cozening: cheating.

craft: guile.

crosses (n.): adversities.

crossly: adversely.

cry: 3.2.102: (a) summon;
  (b) proclaim.

cunning: 1.3.163: (a) skilfully-
  made; (b) requiring skill.

current (adj.): 1.3.231: valid.

date: 5.2.91: phase.

dastard: cowardly assailant.

dateless: ever-protracted.

dead: (i: 3.2.79:) deathly;
  (ii: 4.1.10:) fatal.

dear: (i: 1.1.130: a) costly;
  (b) dire; (ii: 1.3.151:) dire;
  (iii: 1.3.286; 2.1.57-8:) of
  great value.

deceivable: deceitful.

defend: 1.3.18: forbid.

degenerate: false to his rank.

degree: manner; **degree in
  hope**: object of hope; **in any
  fair degree**: 1.1.80: at any
  proper level.

depose: (i: 1.3.30:) examine on
  oath; (ii: 3.2.150: a) depose;
  (b) lay low.

depress: bring low; humble.

design (n.): project; procedure.

design (vb.): indicate;
  designate.

determinate: bring to an end.

detested: detestable.

digressing: transgressing.

direct: 1.1.205: regulate.

discomfortable: disheartening.

dispark: ruin hunting-ground.

dispatch: 4.1.243: hurry.

dispose of: make arrangements
  for.

distaff-women: spinning-
  women.

divine (vb.): prophesy.

divine (adj.): (i: 1.1.38: a)
  immortal; (b) God-given;
  (ii: 5.5.12:) theological.

double: 3.2.21: forked.

doubt: 3.4.69: feared.

draymen: cart-drivers.

dress: (i: 3.4.56, 73:) cultivate;
  (ii: 5.5.80:) groom.

dug (n.): udder: breast.

duty: 3.3.48, 76, 188: homage;
  deference.

eager: 1.1.49: (a) sharp;
  (b) keen.

ear (fig.): 3.3.34: aperture.

ear (vb.): 3.2.212: plough.

Eden: garden of Adam and Eve.

effeminate: 5.3.10: (a) self-
  indulgent; (b) perverse.

embassage belong to: mission
  concern.

endowments: properties.

enfranchisement: (i: 1.3.90:) liberation; (ii: 3.3.114:) restoration of rights.
engaoled: imprisoned.
ensue: follow.
entreated: 3.1.37: treated.
envy (n.): malice.
erned: grieved.
events: 2.1.214: consequences.
exactly: precisely.
except (vb.): take exception to.
exchequer: treasury.
exclaim (n.): outcry.
exeunt (Latin): they go out.
exit: he or she goes out.
expedience: speed.
expedient (adj.): speedy.
extinct: extinguished.
extremity: **in extremity**: to the utmost.
eye of heaven: 1.3.275: (a) sun; (b) God's observation.

faced (vb.): countenanced.
faint (vb. and adj.): 2.1.297; 2.2.32: (be) faint-hearted; **faintly**: 1.3.281; 5.3.103: faint-heartedly.
fall (vb.): 3.4.104: drop; **fall to**: 5.5.98: eat.
fantastic: imagined.
farm (vb.): sell the right to tax; **in farm**: to tax.
favour (n.): (i: 4.1.168: a) face; (b) act of good will; (ii: 5.3.18:) token of support.
fealty: loyalty.
fearful: (i: 2.1.263; 2.4.11:) frightening; (ii: 3.2.110; 3.3.73:) timorous.
fell (adj.): cruel.

female (adj.): 3.2.114: (a) soft; (b) weak.
fetch: 1.1.97: derive.
finis (Latin): the end.
figure (n.): image.
firmament: starry sky.
flatter: (i: 2.1.87:) try to please obsequiously; (ii: 2.1.89:) speciously inspire with hope; **flatter with**: 2.1.88: fawn upon.
Flint Castle: castle near Chester.
foil (n.): setting for a jewel.
fond: (i: 5.1.101: a) foolish; (b) tender; (ii: 5.2.95, 101:) foolish.
fondly (i: 3.2.9:) tenderly; (ii: 3.3.185; 4.1.72:) foolishly.
for: (e.g. at: 1.3.127; 1.4.12; 1.4.43, 52:) because; **for me**: 1.4.6: for my part; **for that**: 1.3.125: because; **for why**: 5.1.46: (a) what's more; (b) because.
forbearance: abstinence.
fore-run: 2.4.15: precede; **fore-run with**: 3.4.28: heralded by.
forfend: forbid.
frantic: mad.
free: 1.3.115: unconstrained.
fretted: 3.3.167: formed by erosion.

gage: 1.1.69, 146; 4.1.25, etc.: pledge, e.g. glove or hood; **in gage**: as pledge;
under gage: as standing challenges.
galled: made sore.
Gaunt: Ghent.
glasses: 1.3.208: (a) windows; (b) mirrors.

Glendo'r: Glendower
(Glyndwr), Welsh leader.
glistering: glittering.
glose: talk speciously.
gnarling: snarling.
Golgotha: 4.1.144: (a) 'skull-
place'; (b) burial-ground; (c)
site of Crucifixion.
gorget: throat-armour.
grace: 3.3.181: honour.
graft (vb.): fix scion to stock.
great: 2.1.228: swollen with
emotion.
grief: 1.3.258: (a) hardship; (b)
suffering.
gripe: 2.1.189; 3.3.80: (a) seize;
(b) grasp tightly.

habiliments of war: armour.
Hallowmas: Feast of All Saints,
Nov. 1st.
hap: fortune.
happily: 5.3.22: (a) by chance;
(b) happily.
happy: 3.1.9: fortunate.
hardly: (i: 2.4.2:) with
difficulty; (ii: 4.1.164:)
scarcely.
haste: **in haste whereof**: to
hasten which.
hateful: full of hatred.
haught-insulting: proudly
insolent.
haviour: conduct.
head: 1.1.97: source.
heaviness: melancholy.
heavy: (i: 1.2.50: a) weighty;
(b) grave; (ii: 2.2.30:) deeply;
(iii: 2.2.32: a) weighty;
(b) grievous; (iv: 3.2.196;
3.3.8; 3.4.2; 5.1.47:) sad;

(v: 4.1.66: a) weightily;
(b) gravely.
height: 1.1.189: high rank.
heir: 2.2.63: offspring.
Her'ford: Hereford.
hie (vb.): hurry.
high-stomached: haughty.
high-way: main road.
his: (e.g. at 1.1.194, 4.1.267:) its.
hollowed: yelled.
humour (n.): temperament.
humoured: entertained.

idly: (i: 3.3.171:) foolishly; (ii:
5.2.25:) casually.
ill-left: poorly equipped.
imp out: mend.
impeach: 1.1.170, 189: discredit;
disparage.
impresse: (It. *impresa*:) heraldic
emblem.
incontinent (adv.): at once.
indifferent: impartial.
infection: 2.1.44: (a) contagious
disease; (b) evil influence.
inhabitable: 1.1.65: uninhabitable.
inherit: (i: 1.1.85:) impart to;
(ii: 2.1.83:) receive.
injurious: 1.1.91: obnoxious.
insatiate: insatiable.
intelligence: information.
interchangeably: (i: 1.1.146:)
reciprocally; (ii: 5.2.98:)
mutually.
ire: anger.

Jack o'th'clock: toy man to
strike a clock-bell.
jade (n.): unruly horse.
jar (vb.): 5.5.51: (a) tick; (b)
enforce.

jauncing: 5.5.94: (a) jogging;
(b) prancing.

jest (vb.): revel.

Jewry: **stubborn Jewry**: Judea,
land of Jews resisting
Christianity.

journeyman: 1.3.274: (a) day-
labourer; (b) traveller.

joy (vb.): 5.6.26: enjoy.

kern: Irish soldier.

kindred of: kinship with.

knave: 2.2.96: (a) lad; (b) fellow.

knot (n.): 3.4.46: (a) patterned
area of garden; (b) social bonds.

lance (vb.): cut, to vent.

large: **at large**: in full.

largess: **liberal largess**: lavish
expenditure.

last: 1.1.131: recently.

league: **keep a league**: remain
allies.

learn: 4.1.120: teach.

leg: **make a leg**: bow deeply.

lending: **in name of lending**:
as advance payment.

let him be: 1.1.59: as if he
were.

letter-patent: official document.

lewd: 1.1.90: (a) improper;
(b) illicit.

liberal: unrestrained.

lief: gladly.

liege: lord.

life: **pain of life**: peril of loss of
life.

light (vb.): 1.1.82: dismount.

light (adv.): **sets it light**: treats
it as trivial.

lighten: 3.3.69: flash.

lineal: hereditary.

lineaments: lineage.

linger: prolong.

lining: 1.4.61: (a) contents;
(b) lining-cloth.

lodge: beat down.

look upon: 4.1.237: observe as
spectator; **look what**: 1.1.87:
(a) whatever; (b) see, what;
look when: 1.3.243: expect
that.

lour: frown; **louring**: looming.

lusty: vigorous.

maim (n.): injury.

make: 5.3.89: do.

manage (n.): (i: 1.4.39:) arrangements; (ii: 3.3.179:) control.

manage (vb.): wield.

manner: **in manner**: so to speak.

manual seal: authorised warrant.

map: epitome.

marry: 1.4.16: (a) by St. Mary;
(b) indeed.

Mars: Roman war-god.

mean (adj.): common.

means: 2.1.39: assets.

measure (n.): (i: 1.2.26:) extent;
(ii: 1.3.291:) stately dance;
(iii: 3.4.7, 8: a) dance;
(b) moderation.

measure our confines: traverse
my land.

meat: food.

meet (adj.): suitable.

men of war: soldiers.

merely: 2.1.243: purely.

merit: (i: 1.3.156:) reward;
(ii: 5.6.18:) worth.

metres: 2.1.19: (a) songs;
(b) poems.

mettle: 1.2.23: (a) essence; (b) semen.

minister (n.): agent.

mistake: (i: 3.3.15:) mis-apprehend; (ii: 3.3.17: a) sin; (b) wrongly assume.

model (n.): (i: 1.2.28, 3.2.153:) copy; (ii: 3.4.42:) small-scale copy; (iii: 5.1.11:) ruined site.

moe: more (in number).

monarchise: play the monarch.

mortal: (i: 1.1.177:) human; (ii: 2.1.152; 3.2.21:) deadly.

motive: 1.1.193: instrument (here tongue).

moveables: portable property.

naked: 1.2.31: (a) defenceless; (b) obvious.

native: 3.2.25: by right of birth.

nea'r: nearer.

next: 1.4.4: nearest.

nicely: 2.1.84: (a) subtly; (b) fussily.

noble (n.): 1.1.88: coin or sum (one-third of £1).

noblesse: nobility.

noisome: harmful.

note (n.): 1.1.43: reproach.

nothing less: anything but.

object (vb.): allege.

obscene: foul.

occident: west.

office: (i: 1.3.256; 2.1.47; 4.1.177:) function; (ii: 2.2.136:) service; (iii: 4.1.5:) deed; **offices**: 1.2.69: servants' quarters.

one: **in one**: 1.1.182: united.

order (vb.): 5.3.140: direct.

or...or: 1.1.93: either . . . or.

ostentation: display.

out-dared: cowed.

out-faced: stared down.

over-proud: too luxuriant.

owe: 4.1.185: own; have.

pain: **on pain of life**: with a death-penalty for defaulting.

pale (n.): 3.4.40: (a) fence; (b) enclosure.

palsy: muscular weakness or paralysis.

parle: 1.1.192; 3.3.33: (a) talk during a truce; (b) trumpet-call to such talk.

partial slander: alleged bias.

partialize: 1.1.120: render one-sided.

party: side.

party-verdict: one share in a joint verdict.

passage: 1.3.272: (a) wandering; (b) travel.

passenger: passer-by.

pawn (n.): 1.1.74; 4.1.70: challenger's symbol: gage of battle; **broking pawn**: being a pledge in a pawn-shop.

peace: **hold thy peace**: be silent.

peaceful: 3.2.125: unopposed.

pelican: bird said to feed its young with its blood.

pelting: paltry; poor.

pérspective: 2.2.18: (here) many-faceted image.

Phaeton: 'Shiner': doomed charioteer of the sun.

piece . . . out: lengthen.

pill (vb.): plunder.

pine (vb.):(i: 3.2.209:) languish; (ii: 5.1.77:) afflict.

pitch (n.): highest point of falcon's flight.

plaining: lamentation.

plaint: sad plea.

planted: established.

Plashie: Pleshey, Woodstock's estate in Essex.

plated: steel-plated.

points: at all points: completely.

Pomfret: Pontefract Castle, Yorkshire.

pompous: splendidly-clad.

Port: le Port Blanc: Port le Blanc, Brittany.

portcullised: guarded by hoistable grill.

possessed: (i: 2.1.107:) owner of the crown; (ii: 2.1.108:) driven by an evil spirit.

post (n.): 2.2.103: fast messengers.

post (vb.): 1.1.56; 3.4.90: hasten.

post (adv.): 5.2.112: rapidly.

postern: small door.

post-haste: speedily.

power: 2.2.123; 3.2.186, 211; 5.3.140: army.

precedent: evidence.

presence: 1.3.289: reception-room at court; **in presence**: 4.1.62: present.

presently: promptly.

press (vb.): 3.2.58: conscript; **press to death**: kill by heaping weights on a victim.

prevent: forestall.

prevention: thwarting.

prick (vb.): urge; incite.

process: progress.

prodigy: monstrous offspring.

profane (vb.): (i: 1.3.59:) misuse; (ii: 1.4.13:) defile; (iii: 3.3.81:) commit sacrilege.

profane (adj.): 2.3.88; 5.1.25: sacrilegious.

proof: 1.3.73: strongest steel.

property: identity.

purchase: acquire.

purge: 1.1.153: expel.

quite (vb.): requite; repay.

ragg'd: ragged: 2.1.70: galled; **raggèd**: 5.5.21: rugged.

rankle: irritate.

ravel: unravel; open out.

Ravenspurgh: port on River Humber in Yorkshire.

raw: inexperienced.

raze . . . out: obliterate.

rebuke: **Gaunt's rebukes**: rebuffs for Gaunt.

receipt: sum received.

record (n.): 1.1.30: witness.

recreant (n.): 1.2.53: coward.

recreant (adj.): (i: 1.1.144:) false to his faith; (ii: 1.3.106, 11: a) cowardly; (b) faithless.

refuge (vb.): rationalise.

regard (n.): consideration.

regreet: greet; salute.

rehearse: 5.3.128: (a) recite; (b) repeat.

remember: 1.3.269: remind.

repair: return.

repeal (vb.): recall from exile.

respect: 2.1.25: (a) concern; (b) aspect.

rest: 2.2.57: remainder.

restful: peaceful.

retired: 2.2.46: led back.

return (vb.): 1.3.122: report to.

reversion: in reversion:
(i: 1.4.35:) prospectively;
(ii: 2.2.38:) prospective.

rheum: excess fluid, e.g. ocular.

rib (fig.): wall.

rid: 5.4.11: eliminate; **rid me of:** free me from.

right (n.): 2.1.190, 201; 2.3.119: entitlement; **right** (adv.): 1.1.46: righteously.

rightly: 2.2.18: (a) from the front; (b) properly.

roan: of mixed colour.

roundly: 2.1.122: (a) freely; (b) boldly.

rouse his wrongs: drive out his wrongers.

royalties: 2.1.190; 2.3.119; 3.3.113: rights granted by the ruler.

rub (n.): obstacle.

rude: coarse; rough.

rue (vb.): repent.

rug-headed: shaggy-haired.

run: (i: 2.1.122:) move; (ii: 2.1.123:) remove.

ruth: pity.

Sacrament: Holy Mass.

safe: 5.3.41: harmless.

Saint Lambert's Day: Sept. 17th.

scope: (i: 3.3.112:) object; (ii: 3.3.140, 141:) opportunity.

scruple: doubt.

seat: (i: 2.1.41, 120; etc.:) throne; (ii: 4.1.140:) place.

secure: heedless; **securely:** (i: 1.3.97:) confidently; (ii: 2.1.266:) heedlessly.

self: 1.2.23: same; **self and vain conceit:** foolish egotism.

self-borne: borne for oneself, not for the King.

senseless conjuration: 3.2.23: (a) injunction to the insentient; (b) inane invocation.

set (vb.): 4.1.57: beset; **sets it light;** deems it little.

several: respective; separate.

shadow: (i: 2.2.14:) illusory form; (ii: 4.1.292: a) enactment; (b) dark mood; (iii: 4.1.293-4:) image.

sheer: pure.

shrewd: sharp.

sift: find out from.

signory: estate.

silly: simple-minded.

sirra: (to inferior:) mister, fellow.

six: at six and seven: in confusion.

slander: 5.6.35: disgrace; **slander of his blood:** disgrace to his lineage; **a partial slander:** an alleged bias.

sly: stealthy.

smooth (vb.): gloss over.

soft (interj.): wait.

solicit: importune.

sometime (adj.): 5.1.37: former; **sometime(s)** (adv.): formerly.

sooth: 3.3.136: (here) flattery.

sore (adv.): grievously.

sort: (i: 4.1.246:) gang; (ii: 5.5.11:) class.

sounded: 1.1.8: elicited from.

sport: entertainment.

spot (n. and vb.): 1.1.175; 3.2.134: disgrace; stain.

spotted: sin-stained.
sprightfully: spiritedly.
stagger (vb.): cause to reel.
stand on: be contingent on.
stand out: hold out;
   stand...upon: be incumbent
   on.
stars: **fair stars**: noble birth.
state: (i: e.g. at 1.3.190; 3.2.72,
   117, 163: a) government;
   (b) majesty; (ii: 3.4.27:)
   politics; (iii: 4.1.192:) status;
   (iv: 4.1.252:) royalty.
stay (vb.): 1.3.4; 2.1.289: await.
sterling: **be sterling**: have value;
   be current.
stews: brothels.
still: 2.1.22; 3.2.62: constantly;
   still-breeding: ever-multiplying.
stir (n.): activity.
stooping duty: submissive
   kneeling.
stop (the ear): render deaf.
stranger (adj.): alien; foreign.
streaming: causing to float in
   the wind.
strewed: strewn with rushes.
strike: 2.1.266: (a) furl sails;
   (b) hit out.
string: 5.5.46: stringed
   instrument.
subscribe: sign someone up to
   pay.
substitute: deputy.
sue...livery: seek legal control
   of lands.
suffer: (i: 2.1.164; 3.4.48:)
   tolerate; (ii: 2.1.267:)
   undergo.
suggest: 1.1.101; 3.4.75:
   (a) incite; (b) tempt.

sullen: 1.3.227, 265; 5.6.48: (a)
   melancholy; (b) sluggish.
sullens: 2.1.139: (a) melancholy;
   (b) sulkiness.
supplant: root out.
sureties: guarantors.
sweet (n.): (i: 2.1.13:) sugary
   confection; (ii: 3.2.13:)
   fragrance.
sympathize: respond
   sympathetically to.
sympathy: 4.1.33: equality in
   rank.

tane: (i: 5.1.53:) issued;
   (ii: 5.2.97:) taken; (iii: 5.6.4:)
   captured.
tapped out: drawn off.
tardy-apish: 2.1.22: tardily
   imitative.
tear (vb.): **torn**: 3.3.83:
   wounded.
teeming: fruitful; productive.
temper: refined steel.
tend: 2.1.32: pertain.
'tend: 4.1.199: attend.
tender (vb.): (i: 1.1.32:) cherish;
   (ii: 2.3.41:) offer.
tender (adj.): 2.3.42:
   inexperienced.
tends . . . to: 2.1.232: concerns.
tenement: rented property.
thrive to beat: succeed in
   beating.
throw: 4.1.57: cast dice.
tied: 1.1.63: obliged.
time: 1.3.220: season; **mortal
   times**: men's lives..
timeless: untimely.
toiled with: exhausted by.
touch: 1.3.165: fingering.

trade (n.): 3.3.156:
(a) commerce; (b) travel.

trespass (n.): 1.1.138; 5.2.89:
crime.

triumph (n.): 5.2.52; 5.3.14:
public show, e.g. tournament.

trow: 2.1.218: (a) believe;
(b) trust.

true: 1.3.86; 2.1.192; 5.3.145:
loyal.

truth: 1.3.19; 4.1.171; 5.2.44:
loyalty; fidelity.

try: put to the test.

twain (n.): two.

twain (vb.): 5.3.134: divide:
hence, weaken.

unavoided: unavoidable.

uncivil: barbarous.

uncontrolled: unrestricted.

undeaf (vb.): restore hearing to.

underbearing (n.): endurance.

undo: 4.1.203: (a) divest;
(b) ruin.

unfelt: intangible.

unfurnished: 1.2.68: lacking
tapestry, etc.

ungracious: graceless; profane.

unhappy (vb.): 3.1.10: make
(a) unhappy; (b) unfortunate.

unpeopled: 1.2.69: without
servants.

unstaid: unruly.

unthrift: spendthrift.

unthrifty: profligate; feckless.

untruth: disloyalty.

urge (vb.): 3.1.4; 4.1.271; 5.4.5:
insist on.

vantage: (i: 1.3.218:) profit;
(ii: 5.3.132:) advantage.

venom (n.): 2.1.157: (a) poison;
(b) venomous snakes.

venom (adj.): 2.1.19: poisonous.

verge: (i: 1.1.93: a) border;
(b) horizon; (ii: 2.1.102: a)
circle of metal; (b) area
around the court.

viol: stringed instrument.

wail: lament.

want (n.): 1.4.51; 3.2.175: need.

want (vb.): 3.3.179; 3.4.16: lack.

wanton: (i: 1.3.214:) lively;
(ii: 5.1.101: a) excessive;
(b) frivolous; (iii: 5.3.10:)
feckless; **play the wantons**:
frolic; trifle.

warder: baton; truncheon.

waste: 2.1.103: (a) waste ground;
(b) spoliation.

watch (n.): 5.5.52: (a) minute-
signs on a dial; (b) clock face;
watches: 5.5.52: periods of vigil.

watch (vb.): 2.1.77: (a) stay
awake; (b) keep guard.

watching: 2.1.78: sleeplessness.

waxen: as if it were wax.

way: 3.2.179: cause.

whencesoever: from wherever
he is.

where: 3.2.185: whereas.

wherefore: why.

while: 1.3.122: until.

will (n.): 2.1.28: desire.

win: 2.3.162: persuade.

wink: close dazzled eyes.

wishtly: 5.4.7: (a) longingly;
(b) intently.

witnessing: presaging.

wit's regard: intelligent
awareness.

wont: accustomed.
worthy: apt.
wot: know.
wrack (n.): shipwreck.

yoke: 2.1.291: (a) wooden shoulder-frame to pair oxen or bear pails; (b) burden.
zeal: moral fervour.